Feed *the* Birds

Feed *the* Birds

Attract and Identify
196 Common North American Birds

CHRIS EARLEY

endorsed by the

CANADIAN WILDLIFE
FEDERATION

FIREFLY BOOKS

A FIREFLY BOOK

Published by Firefly Books Ltd. 2019

First printing

Library of Congress Control Number: 2019937754

Library and Archives Canada Cataloguing in Publication

Title: Feed the birds : attract and identify 196 common North American birds / Chris Earley.

Other titles: Attract and identify one hundred ninety-six North American birds

Names: Earley, Chris, 1968- author.

Description: "Endorsed by the Canadian Wildlife Federation." | Includes bibliographical references and index.

Identifiers: Canadiana 20190085843 | ISBN 9780228102014 (softcover)

Subjects: LCSH: Bird attracting—North America—Handbooks, manuals, etc. | LCSH: Birds—Feeding and feeds—North America—Handbooks, manuals, etc. | LCSH: Birds—North America—Identification. | LCSH: Bird watching—North America.

Classification: LCC QL681 .E27 2019 | DDC 598.097—dc23

Published in the United States by
Firefly Books (U.S.) Inc.
P.O. Box 1338, Ellicott Station
Buffalo, New York 14205

Published in Canada by
Firefly Books Ltd.
50 Staples Avenue, Unit 1
Richmond Hill, Ontario L4B 0A7

Cover and interior design: Kimberley Young
Illustrations on pages 80–87: Wayne Kelusky
Illustrations on pages 50, 51, 73: George A. Walker
Maps: George A. Walker

Front Cover: John Van Decker / Alamy Stock Photo: main image; FotoRequest / Shutterstock: bottom left; Oli Moorman / Shutterstock: bottom center; Tim Zurowski / Shutterstock: bottom right

Spine: John L. Absher / Shutterstock

Back Cover: Chris Earley (right); Andalyne Tofflemire (bottom left)

Printed in China

Canadä We acknowledge the financial support of the Government of Canada.

Dedication

To Dr. Gard Otis, a long-time birder, and to Dr. Shelley Hunt, a beginning but already competent one. Thank you both for the nature knowledge you have shared with me and the hundreds of undergrads in your classes. You have helped many better understand our ecosystems and that is a gift to everyone.

Acknowledgments

This book could not have been possible without the talent, generosity and keen eyes of the photographers. Thank you! Thanks also to the whole team at Firefly and especially Lionel Koffler and Michael Worek for putting up with me all of these years and all of these books.

Contents

IDENTIFYING BIRDS

Introduction

W HEN I WAS 7 years old, my family moved to a new house. It was situated on the end of a quiet street, and our backyard sloped into a ravine that led into a conservation area full of frogs, toads, turtles and butterflies. I was already known as an animal lover, but this new environment helped me become what is known in many small towns in North America as "that nature kid." I was the one who was called when a friend had a giant cecropia moth on his screen door or when an aunt had a snake in her window well or when a neighbor found an orphaned raccoon kit.

ABOVE   A Red-breasted Nuthatch and a
Black-capped Chickadee share a peanut feeder.

The natural world had always been magical to me, but that magic increased 10-fold when my parents put up a bird feeder outside our kitchen window. Amazing! It was like having a fish tank where the fish kept on changing. A Black-capped Chickadee would grab a sunflower seed and then fly off while a White-breasted Nuthatch worked away on the suet tied to a tree trunk. The noisy Blue Jays chased everyone away until the loud "chow" of an arriving Red-bellied Woodpecker warned them that the real boss was about to arrive. I can remember the winter day when a flock of brilliantly colored Pine Grosbeaks flew in and spent the afternoon in the various trees and shrubs in my yard.

Whether it was the brightness of a Northern Cardinal, the gregarious habits of the American Goldfinches or the plump form of a Fox Sparrow, there was always something to look at and wonder about.

Now I have my own house, and here I am, sitting at my kitchen table writing this book as I watch the birds at my feeders outside the window. Not much has changed. I hope that the following pages inspire you to not only set up your own feeders but also really watch the birds in your yard to see just how amazingly adapted they are to their environment. They will hopefully help strengthen your link to our incredible natural world.

Two hummers compete for a spot at the feeder.

TOP   A suet feeder entices a Pileated Woodpecker out into the open.

Why Feed Birds?

Since you are reading this book, you probably already know that watching birds is awesome! We have always been fascinated by their ability to fly, their musical songs and their brilliant colors. Bird feeders allow us to entice these feathered marvels out into the open, so we can see them, identify them and watch them live their lives.

As you watch birds, look for each species' individual adaptations for survival. The propping ability of a woodpecker's tail, the strength of a cardinal's beak, the maneuverability of a hummingbird's flight — all these features help each bird live in its own special niche.

Binoculars and a tally sheet for Project Feederwatch.

Citizen Science for the Birds

There are lots of ways to learn more about the birds at your feeders and contribute data to science projects. If you have children in your house, this could tie into a science fair project, too.

Project Feederwatch

Project Feederwatch (feederwatch.org) is the perfect way to contribute your sightings to science. The Cornell Lab of Ornithology analyzes this data to uncover trends in bird populations across North America. You count the birds that come to your feeder over a two-day period every week. The goal is to record the highest number of each species that you can see at once. This is a great project for children to be involved in because they can help with the counts.

eBird and iNaturalist

eBird.com and iNaturalist.org/iNaturalist.ca (as well as .org) are sites where you can record your bird sightings, whether it be in your backyard or beyond. You can also use these sites to keep a record of all the birds you have seen in your life as well as find out which birds have been seen near you and which birds you might see when you travel to a new place. Check it out!

Christmas Bird Counts and the Great Backyard Bird Count

Every December, there are Christmas Bird Counts across North America. Join your local birders on one of these, and see what is around your area while socializing with like-minded bird lovers. There are Christmas Bird Counts for Kids events and the Great Backyard Bird Count, too. You can find more information at audubon.org/conservation/science/christmas-bird-count, birdscanada.org/volunteer/gbbc/ and audubon.org/conservation/about-great-backyard-bird-count.

Other Citizen Science Projects

There are many other citizen science projects that relate to birds. These sites list many opportunities for you to contribute: see www.birdscanada.org/volunteer and www.americanornithology.org/content/citizen-science-projects.

Participants count birds during a Christmas Bird Count.

Involving Kids in Birding

Starting Early: Toddlers

Really, they can do it! You just need to modify some of the things that every parent does with their kids. Instead of asking your toddler, "What does a pig say?" why not ask, "What does a crow say?" That will impress your birding friends! Other great sounds for toddlers to mimic are Mourning Doves and Black-capped Chickadees.

You can also put up a bird feeder outside your kitchen window, which your toddler can watch from his or her highchair. While doing some dishes, I once looked outside through our kitchen sink window and saw a Blue Jay at the feeder. I turned to my son, Nathan, then two years old, who was sitting beside the back deck window in his highchair, and asked, "Can you say Blue Jay?" He looked outside and promptly replied "Dove." I said, "No, that is a Blue Jay. Can you say Blue Jay?" He looked at me and said, "Dove!"

We then had quite a heated argument of "Blue Jay!" "Dove!" Blue Jay!" "Dove!" Until I walked over to him, pointed to the Blue Jay and said in a very loud voice "Blue Jay!" No kid of mine was going to incorrectly identify a Blue Jay, no matter how old he was.

Nathan then pointed to the ground under the feeder (which I couldn't see from the window over the sink), where there were eight Mourning Doves. He screamed "Dove! Cooo Cooo Cooo Cooo!" So, yes, even a two-year-old can make the correct identification despite the incorrect instructions from his father.

Everything Is New: Preschoolers

Nothing beats the curiosity of a three- or four-year-old. The backyard bird feeder can be the focal point for teaching your child about field marks and feeding strategies. Unfortunately, binoculars really don't work well for very young children because they can't hold them still enough and have trouble finding the birds when looking through the lenses.

I suggest that you go to the hardware store and buy two plastic connectors (the ones you would use to connect 1½- or 2-inch PVC piping) and make a pair of binos. It's very easy to do: simply attach the connectors, side by side, using a strong tape, such as duct tape. Not only are these binos light and easy to handle, but the optics are super clear!

Kids can use their homemade binos and feel like they are doing what you are doing. But don't despair if they are more focused on the insects at their feet than on the birds. Remember, the little finch you are looking at is likely out

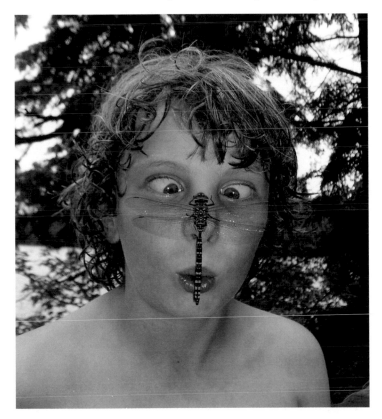

My son, Nathan, was always more interested in bugs than birds when he was younger.

My daughter, Skye, paints a cardinal that we now use as part of our outside Christmas decorations.

of the child's bino range, whereas the praying mantis or butterfly is right there in front of him or her.

Encourage their interest in anything natural, such as insects, frogs, wildflowers or even pine cones. A healthy curiosity for other parts of nature is wonderful and may translate to birds when they get older. Be patient!

Project Time: Ages 5 to 8

You can do some fun bird-watching projects with kids in this age group. When Nathan was six we started to make his own field guide. I set aside an old photographic guide and put a bunch of lined pages in a small binder. Every time Nathan saw a new bird species, we would find it in the guide, cut out the photo and glue it onto one of the lined pages in the binder. He would then write out the name of the bird at the top of the page. Pretty soon he had a booklet full of the birds he had seen.

Think about the type of projects that your child likes to do and relate them to birds. Starting a feather collection, constructing a bird out of building blocks or making a bird collage using old magazines are just a few ideas your child may enjoy.

Science: Ages 9 to 12

Participating in Project Feederwatch (see page 10) is perfect for this age group. My kids and I even make it a bit competitive: Who can see the greatest number of, for example, Dark-eyed Juncos at once during a two-day period? It's great to hear a triumphant "Yes!" coming from the next room when the sheet is checked and a higher number is written in.

Interest in birds at this age can wax and wane, so I suggest leaving the Project Feederwatch sheets on the kitchen table with a pen during each count period. This allows budding scientists to add to the list randomly, rather than try to schedule sessions and have everyone sit together to watch. You'll be surprised how many additions that aren't your own are on the sheet at the end of each count period.

Another good research project for this age group is to attend a Christmas Bird Count for Kids event (see page 11). These events are great because there are other kids doing the same thing!

Hand-feeding (see pages 44–45) is also a pleaser for this age group. You may not have time to train your own birds, but you can likely find a nearby park, nature center or conservation area that already has friendly birds waiting for you to visit.

The Challenge: Teenagers

So now it gets tricky. While some teenagers might be cool with continuing their interest in birds, others are mortified when you bring your binoculars out of your backpack. The best thing to do is let the teenager decide when birding might be okay, but don't be afraid to make offers they can't refuse: missing some school for a hiking trip, for example, might make it worthwhile for them. You can also try to set up a special event, such as visiting a bird banding station or going on a public owl prowl, and let them bring a friend. Or you might suggest a science fair project that uses your bird feeder. Be persistent with offers but not forceful. All those "Noes" may someday change to a "Yes."

Photography

It is a natural step from observing to "capturing" your feeder birds. Photography lets you combine your inner hunter with your inner artist, and the result is a memory you can put onto paper or screen. The best cameras for this have a good zoom feature or are DSLR cameras with a good telephoto lens. Many camera stores and nature centers offer courses in wildlife photography for beginners, and these can help get you started.

Lunch to go! A friend of mine captured this comical shot of a young Ruby-throated Hummingbird. The hummer had been feeding on some bee balm when one of the florets came off on its beak. The bird flew in fast, tight circles for a few seconds before it could figure out how to ditch the petaled hat!

If you only have a cell phone camera, you can still have fun taking photos. Hand-feeding birds will bring them close enough for a good phone-camera shot. But do not zoom in on your screen before taking the photo; it is better to take a photo and then zoom in with your phone's editing features.

Phone videos of hand-feeding birds are even more fun. Try capturing a chickadee grabbing a sunflower seed with your slow-motion feature — they turn out great! You can also try attaching your phone directly to your bird feeder and turning on the video feature to get some superb close-up footage to share with friends and family on social media.

The day I wrote the Pileated Woodpecker pages for this book, I was frustrated because I had never attracted one to my feeders. The next day, during a family party, this female showed up! I got to show her off to everyone and even grabbed this photo. Having a shot like this will bring a smile to your face each time you see it because you know the whole story that goes with it.

My Mourning Doves always land on the top of my hopper feeder, walk to the roof edge and then jump onto the platform to feed. But during a recent ice storm, this landing method turned into a skiing session! My camera allowed me to catch their sliding experiences.

1
Feeding Wild Birds

I have four different types of feeders on one of my poles, and here you can see seven different bird species visiting at the same time.

OFFERING A WIDE variety of foods in a wide variety of feeders will increase the diversity of your feathered visitors. There are many shapes and makes of bird feeders and different seeds available; your local nature store will offer many choices. Here I review the main types of feeders and foods and the benefits of each.

Does Bird-Feeding Harm Birds?

This is a complicated question, but, overall, bird-feeding does not harm birds. It may surprise you to learn that only about 10 percent of most feeder birds' diets are from feeders. Studies have shown that wild birds that do not have access to feeders have the same survivability as those with access to feeders, except when there are extremely cold conditions

This American Goldfinch is showing signs of "finch eye disease," also known as mycoplasmal conjunctivitis. When you see a sick bird such as this one, you should clean your feeder very thoroughly and more frequently than usual.

or ice storms. In those cases, the birds with access to feeders have a better chance of survival.

Another study showed that a bird's overall health was better if it had access to feeders. These birds had higher antioxidant levels, faster feather growth and lower stress levels. Some species even had better body condition and greater immunity to infections and diseases. But the study did show that there was a higher rate of disease transmission among the birds that fed at feeders. This makes sense: a higher concentration of birds means that diseases can spread more easily.

However, another study showed that even though there were more diseases present around feeders, the birds that visited them were better at fighting the diseases because they were in better condition than birds without access to

An American Tree Sparrow braves an ice storm.

feeders. To stop the spread of disease, it is important to use fresh seed and clean your feeders every few weeks, depending on the conditions. If your feeder is visited by many birds, you'll need to wash it more often. The weather is another important consideration: feeders may need to be washed more often when it's hot and humid. Use a 10-percent bleach solution and then rinse the feeders well. Always wash your hands after filling and washing your feeders.

What to Feed

There are lots of different seed mixes out there, so how do you decide what to use? The following are what I consider to be the "Super Six Seed Selections." If you use these in your feeding regime, you will attract a wide variety of bird species to your feeders.

Black Oil Sunflower Seeds

If you can only feed one type of seed, this should be it. It is not only eaten by many bird species, it is often their pre-ferred choice. You can also get this seed without the shells; it is more expensive when shelled, but it has the added bonus of not having shells accumulate under your feeder.

Striped Sunflower Seeds

Though less preferred overall than black oil, the larger, striped sunflower seeds seem to be a favorite of larger birds, such as jays.

Safflower Seeds

This is an interesting seed. Some find that blackbirds, house sparrows, starlings and squirrels don't like it, but other birds do; others find that all birds seem to eat it, and some find that none do! You may have to experiment. At my feeder, I have watched Northern Cardinals and Fox Sparrows eat lots of this seed.

White Millet

Lots of bird species eat this seed, but sparrows and doves seem to especially like it. I put it in my hopper feeder mixed with sunflower and safflower seeds. I also spread it on the ground.

Nyjer Seeds

Sometimes called thistle seed (even though it isn't from a thistle at all), this small black seed is a choice food of many species of finches, including goldfinches, redpolls and siskins.

Peanuts

Peanuts pack a lot of protein and fat, and they come in three main forms: in the shell, without the shell and in a spread (pudding-like) form. Peanuts are a preferred food of woodpeckers, jays, nuthatches, chickadees and titmice. I like to feed peanuts in the shell at a large feeder so I can watch the Blue Jays work at extracting each one. Chickadees and nuthatches prefer to eat shelled peanuts from a mesh feeder.

Other Seeds

Not all seeds are good for birds and some need to be used with special care. While cracked corn is fine and is eaten by quail, doves, jays, sparrows and blackbirds, it can also be a favorite of squirrels. Corn should never be allowed to get wet as it can go bad quickly. Don't offer it or shelled peanuts in a plastic tube feeder where moisture can build up and accelerate fungal growth. Offer corn in small amounts so it is eaten completely each day or two; this will help stop a build up of old corn. Milo (aka sorghum) is a good example of how regional differences can be important considerations for seed selection. In the eastern parts of North America, milo is not a choice food, and so it often goes uneaten and should be avoided. However, in the west, this seed can be added to seed mixes as it is eaten by a variety of birds. Talk to staff at your local bird store to see if milo is eaten in your area before offering it.

A Blue Jay fills its throat with corn kernels. It will likely fly somewhere, hide them and eat them later.

Seed Mixes

Using seed mixes can be a good option for feeding birds, but not all mixes are of high quality, so check the ingredients carefully. Some ingredients of poor mixes, such as wheat, oats, red millet and flax, are usually not preferred foods of backyard birds, and these leftovers may accumulate and attract rodents. Here are two examples of superior mixes containing favorite seeds.

Wild Birds Unlimited Deluxe Blend

Includes: black oil sunflower, striped sunflower, safflower and white millet. This mix has all you need to attract a wide variety of birds. Works well in a hopper feeder, a large tube feeder or spread on the ground. The sunflower and safflower will be especially attractive to chickadees, jays, nuthatches, finches and cardinals. The white millet will bring in sparrows, juncos, towhees, doves and quail.

Canadian Wildlife Federation Vibrance Mix

Includes: black oil sunflower, striped sunflower, safflower and peanut halves. These seeds are choice food for many birds including chickadees, jays, nuthatches, finches and cardinals. The peanut halves will also be prized and can also attract different woodpecker species. This mix works best in a hopper, large mesh or raised platform feeder.

Is it Fresh?

Stored bird seed does not last forever. If you find your seed is in clumps, is moldy and/or smells rancid or is "off," it is time to throw it away. Not only is it less nutritious for your birds, it could be dangerous to their health. Seed that has sprouted or is very old (it may seem either rubbery or dusty) should be discarded as well.

Seed Storage: Do This!

Store your seed in metal garbage cans with metal lids. This will deter mice, which can chew through plastic containers to get to the seed. Depending on how fast you use it, some seeds, such as nyjer, may need to be stored in sealed plastic bags or airtight containers inside the metal garbage can to keep them fresh.

Non-Seed Feeds

Birds eat more than just seeds! Put out a variety of options to attract as many birds as possible to your yard or balcony.

A Pileated Woodpecker visits the carcass of a deer.

Suet

Suet is a must to round off your winter bird-feeding menu. Woodpeckers, jays, nuthatches and chickadees all love it. You can buy premade "suet cakes" or get beef suet directly from your butcher. You can set out suet cakes all year round, and they often come in different "flavors" that incorporate various nuts, seeds, fruits and even mealworms into the suet.

Beef suet is best used in colder weather, when it won't go rancid. Suet mimics what some birds would find when they come across an animal carcass. Ravens, crows, jays and woodpeckers are not above stealing a bit of venison from a wolf kill, for example

Suet/Peanut Butter Spread

If you mix suet, peanut butter and cornmeal, you can make a nutritious spread that many birds enjoy (there are many different recipes to try online). You can buy premade "bark butter" at backyard birding stores as well.

Don't use peanut butter on its own because the oils can sometimes gum up a bird's feathers and result in their no longer being waterproof. Adding cornmeal or wheat flour can help stop this from happening.

A Golden-fronted Woodpecker is eating a peanut butter spread (peanut butter mixed with cornmeal) from a simple homemade feeder.

Fruits and Jellies

You can attract some species of birds to your yard with fruit. Orange halves are particularly attractive to many species of orioles, grosbeaks, tanagers, mockingbirds, thrashers and even woodpeckers. Other fruits you might want to try include melon rinds, cut up apple, grapes, raisins and blueberries.

Jellies, such as grape jelly, may also help attract orioles and nuthatches.

A Cedar Waxwing shares jelly with a Baltimore Oriole.

Nectar

Putting out a sugar–water mixture (nectar) can attract hummingbirds and orioles. The easiest and best way to make this mixture is to boil 4 cups (1 L) of water and then add 1 cup (250 mL) of regular white sugar. Stir until the sugar has disappeared, and let the mixture cool. Leftover formula can be stored in the refrigerator until it is needed (it is good for about a week).

This 4:1 ratio is closest to natural nectar, and white sugar is the only sugar you should use. Do not use other sweeteners, such as maple syrup or honey. And no food coloring should be used: the best feeders are already red to attract hummingbirds

Mealworms

Mealworms are a great offering for birds that may not be attracted to seeds. Bluebirds, mockingbirds and wrens are especially interested in mealworms, which are actually beetle larvae. Try getting some from a local pet store, and see if your birds eat them!

A tiny male Rufous Hummingbird gives us a great view of its body in flight as it stops at a feeder.

BOTTOM Mealworms have attracted a Northern Mockingbird to this feeder.

How to Feed

Ground Feeding

The easiest feeder! Almost all birds will feed from the ground, but some, like doves, quail, turkeys and sparrows, may prefer it. It is best to spread seed in an area where it won't get too wet and go moldy.

Feed: any seed or seed mix

There are seven different bird species in this shot.

Hopper Feeders

Hopper feeders have many benefits. First of all, they usually have a large perching area that allows birds of all sizes to feed. Second, the center of the feeder holds a significant amount of feed, meaning less trips to refill for you. Third, it has a roof that protects the seed and the birds from precipitation. Last but not least, these feeders are easily attached to the top of a pole, or they can be hung from a tree branch or hook.

Feed: seed mixes

A plastic hopper feeder with a colorful Blue Grosbeak and a Northern Cardinal.

RIGHT This large hopper feeder can accommodate many Evening Grosbeaks at once.

Mesh Feeders

These feeders can work like hopper feeders, and they have the added bonus of allowing many birds to be on the actual storage area of the feeder at the same time. They allow plenty of airflow around the seed, but in wet conditions you may have to change the feed if it isn't eaten right away and goes moldy.

Feed: sunflower seeds or peanuts

An entire flock of Black-capped Chickadees has landed on this mesh feeder at once.

FAR LEFT   This fun mesh feeder can accommodate the vertical perching style of woodpeckers, such as this Red-bellied Woodpecker.

TOP LEFT   The bottom tray of this mesh feeder helps prevent spillage, and this male House Finch is using it as a perch.

BOTTOM LEFT   A Purple Finch feeds on black oil sunflower seeds.

This large tube feeder holds a lot of feed and keeps it evenly distributed throughout the feeder, so as the volume gets low, the seed doesn't pile up at the bottom ports only. Here, Common Redpolls and a Black-capped Chickadee are feasting.

BELOW LEFT A Red-winged Blackbird is using the seed tray on the bottom of this tube feeder as a perch.

BELOW CENTER A male Painted Bunting accesses a seed mix.

BELOW RIGHT Tube feeders can hold seed mixes, allowing this Field Sparrow to eat its favorite food — white millet.

Tube Feeders

Tube feeders can store lots of seed and provide small- to medium-sized birds with multiple openings for easy access. They can be used with seed mixes or with one seed type only, depending on the size of the ports. Most have individual ports with small perches, which discourage larger birds. Some tube feeders have a spring system that can be adjusted so you can stop squirrels and heavier birds from getting to the seed (see page 72).

Feed: seed mixes

Peanut Feeders

I find that a feeder that makes my Blue Jays work a bit to get the peanut out is one of my favorites. I like watching them get into different positions to extract each peanut before they fly off to either store or eat it. Some people train their jays to come to their backyard at specific times by just putting out a few peanuts on schedule.

Shelled peanuts are much more accessible to a variety of birds and work best if they are presented in a mesh tube feeder. Suet/peanut butter spreads (see page 26) can be used in cold weather and spread on tree trunks or stuffed into pre-drilled holes in a log. Remember, never use peanut butter on its own, as the oils can gum up a bird's feathers, making them no longer waterproof.

Feed: peanuts

ABOVE LEFT   This is my favorite peanut feeder. The jays can easily take out the peanuts when it is full but have to work harder and harder as the number of peanuts goes down (see page 103).

above right   A mesh peanut feeder is a good choice for holding the peanut pieces that attracted this Black-capped Chickadee.

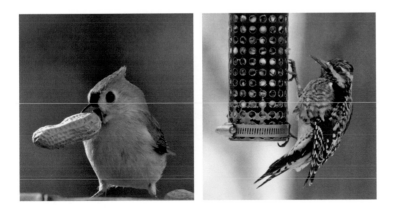

LEFT   Tufted Titmice like peanuts no matter how they are offered! They can even pick up and drill into peanuts in the shell.

RIGHT   Yellow-bellied Sapsuckers may be enticed to a feeder with shelled peanuts.

Platform Feeders

A large homemade platform feeder attracts many Evening Grosbeaks.

Platform feeders are suitable for all species of birds. When combined with a squirrel baffle (see page 72), these feeders allow larger birds or flocks of birds to feed when seed on the ground is being dominated by squirrels. The best platform feeders have a mesh base or many drainage holes, which allow water to drain freely so the seed can dry out and not become moldy.

Feed: seed mixes

This Black-headed Grosbeak is feeding from a small mesh platform feeder.

BOTTOM   A Carolina Wren is using a platform feeder.

Nyjer Feeders

Most nyjer feeders are tube feeders with very small openings that allow smalls seed to be picked out by the birds. This stops the nyjer from blowing away and keeps it protected from rain and snow. Most nyjer feeders have perches, and some of them are made of plastic with tiny ports, while others are made of mesh.

Feed: nyjer

ABOVE LEFT   A Common Redpoll gets nyjer from a mesh tube feeder.

ABOVE CENTER   If House Finches take over your nyjer feeder, you can also provide a feeder that has the ports under the perches. This allows different birds, such as these American Goldfinches and Pine Siskins, to feed but not the heavier, less dexterous House Finches.

ABOVE RIGHT   A nyjer sock is another way to offer this small seed. These American Goldfinches can pull the seed through the openings. Sock feeders are easy to wash, too, as most can go in your washing machine.

A typical nyjer feeder, such as this one, has small openings that prevent spills but allow birds, such as this House Finch, to access the seed. The metal around the ports stops squirrels from chewing through the plastic.

ABOVE A Bushtit samples some suet.

A Red-breasted Nuthatch lays claim to a large northern forest suet feeder. This feeder has extra reinforcements so only the targeted birds can get at the suet. Local American Martens visit it regularly and would take the entire suet chunks if they could.

Suet Feeders

It is best to offer suet in some kind of mesh feeder that allows the birds to peck out pieces but stops squirrels and other mammals from stealing the whole chunk.

Feed: suet and suet cakes

ABOVE LEFT In some areas, European Starlings can quickly devour suet. This upside-down feeder makes it difficult for starlings to get to the suet inside but doesn't stop this Red-bellied Woodpecker.

TOP LEFT A Golden-fronted Woodpecker shows that a place to put your tail is not always necessary!

ABOVE A Hairy Woodpecker on a suet feeder that has an extension to accommodate a woodpecker's tail. This feeder also has a lid that stops ice from forming on the suet.

LEFT Suet can attract birds that don't normally visit seed feeders, such as this Gray Catbird and Yellow-throated Warbler.

Fruit and Jelly Feeders

Feeding fruits and jellies to your backyard birds can as simple as putting out some cut fruit. However, you can also purchase dedicated feeders that can be hung from poles and include perches for the targeted birds.

ABOVE Apples may attract American Robins, Varied Thrushes, House Finches and waxwings.

BOTTOM RIGHT A Gray Catbird eats grape jelly provided in a can attached to a tree trunk.

BOTTOM LEFT This orange half has attracted an American Robin.

RIGHT A Rose-breasted Grosbeak, a Baltimore Oriole and a Red-bellied Woodpecker enjoy oranges and nectar.

Too much of a good thing

Only offer shallow servings of jelly as small birds can get stuck in larger amounts.

A Baltimore Oriole hits the jackpot with these orange slices all to himself.

Nectar Feeders

A very busy nectar feeder!

Nectar feeders are colored red so that harmful red dye need not be added to the formula. Be sure to change the formula every few days or even daily in very hot weather. And wash your nectar feeder weekly; some can even be put in the dishwasher.

TOP LEFT Nectar feeders have their own challenges, such as bees, wasps and ants. Ants can be deterred with an "ant moat," which is built into many feeders.

BOTTOM LEFT If you are patient, you might even get a hummer to land on your hand!

RIGHT Orioles (such as this male Baltimore), tanagers, warblers and other birds may also visit hummingbird feeders to dine on nectar.

Mealworms

Mealworms aren't the greatest climbers, so putting them in a steep-sided metal or glass bowl will keep them from escaping before birds have a chance to taste them.

Three male Eastern Bluebirds get some insect protein on a snowy afternoon.

Other Feeders

There are many other feeders out there for you to try. Check out your local bird/nature store and ask them what success others in your area have had with different designs.

A pair of Carolina Wrens find a seed bell to their liking.

BELOW LEFT A suction cup window feeder can give you great looks at species such as this Eastern Bluebird. If you have many squirrels in your area, this type of feeder may not work for you.

BELOW RIGHT If you can't beat them . . . This fun feeder welcomes squirrels with their own seat and table.

Do-It-Yourself Feeders

Are you considering making a feeder yourself? The following pages explain how to make a good hopper design, but you can also make simple feeders out of plastic bottles or milk cartons — get creative! Be aware, though, that homemade feeders tend to be easily raided by squirrels, so you may want to try your own do-it-yourself baffle, too (see page 73).

TOP LEFT A plastic bottle can be easily converted into a fine-dining establishment for local birds.

TOP RIGHT AND LEFT A log with holes drilled into it or even a pine cone can work as a peanut butter feeder, as shown by this White-breasted Nuthatch and this Verdin. Because the oils from pure peanut butter can be problematic to bird's feathers, be sure to add cornmeal to the peanut butter mixture.

Get creative and use your own individual style.

ABOVE RIGHT   An old peanut butter jar and some ingenuity can combine for a wonderful feeder.

RIGHT   Give the woodworker in your family a challenge and see what they come up with! There are plans for building homemade feeders on pages 80–87.

Reusing plastic has resulted in a feeder, a squirrel baffle and some satisfied chickadees.

LEFT My daughter made this feeder out of a pencil and some craft sticks. I didn't have the heart to tell her that it wouldn't work, so I hung it up anyway. However, as so often happens, she was right all along and the chickadees loved it.

Gray Jays, known for their boldness, are probably the easiest birds to hand-feed. They have been taking human food for centuries, earning them the nickname "camp robber."

Hand-Feeding

Hand-feeding a wild feeder bird is something you never forget. Some birds, like chickadees and titmice, can be enticed fairly easily, while other species are more challenging. To train the birds at your feeder, start by sitting near the feeder without moving very much. Move a little closer to the feeder every day. Next, try standing near the feeder. Finally, put seed in your outstretched hand and see what happens. Sometimes things will go quicker if you block access to the feed in the feeders when you do this, so only the feed in your hand is available to the birds. I also find that standing on one side of the feeder but holding my hand out to the other side gets birds to land on my hand more easily.

TOP LEFT Some blackbirds, like this Brewer's Blackbird, will get bold enough to take handouts in city parks.

Downy Woodpeckers (*above*), White-breasted Nuthatches and Red-breasted Nuthatches (*left*) are frequent hand feeders.

BOTTOM LEFT My daughter's friend covered herself with snow and then sprinkled seed on top. She had a whole flock of redpolls land on her!

BELOW Chickadees are often a birder's first success at hand-feeding.

2
Creating a Bird Friendly Backyard

A backyard that provides all four elements will be most attractive to wildlife.

Backyards for Wildlife

You can make your backyard or garden wildlife friendly by providing four basic needs:

1. Food This includes seeds, fruits, berries and nuts as well as leaves, bark, nectar, pollen, buds and flowers. These foods attract many different species of wildlife, including insects, which in turn attract animals higher up on the food chain, which eat these herbivores. A healthy habitat garden includes members from many different parts of the ecosystem (plant-eaters, predators, scavengers, etc.). Natural foods can be supplemented with bird feeders.

2. Water Obviously needed for drinking, water is also important for a variety of aquatic creatures and plants, which in turn attract birds. A water source such as a small

An American Robin samples a berry from a planted staghorn sumac.

pond is an important environment for animals that live part of their life cycle in the water, such as dragonflies, toads and frogs, so it can be advantageous to incorporate one into your yard, if possible. Birds also use water for bathing, which helps them maintain their feathers.

3. Shelter Whether to protect themselves from the elements or predators or as a space in which to raise their young, birds require shelter, which are an important part of any wildlife garden. There are various ways you can enhance the shelter options in your yard, such as making a brush pile, planting a conifer hedge, adding a shaded arbor or putting up a nest box.

4. Space Some need a little and some need a lot, but all wildlife needs at least some space to survive. But that doesn't mean you need a massive property to help wildlife or attract birds. Small city gardens can be incredibly diverse spaces that include all four of the basic needs of wildlife habitat. Simple things like bird baths, bird houses, container gardens, border shrubs, brush piles or bird feeders don't have to take up a lot of space.

Yard Set-up

1. Feeders: pages 28–43
2. Baffle: pages 72–73
3. Bird box: pages 64–69
4. Hummingbird feeder: page 38
5. Water: pages 59–61
6. Perennial border: pages 52–55
7. Fruiting Shrubs: pages 52–53
8. Conifer or dense bush corridor: pages 62–63
9. Window dots: pages 76–77

Ideally, feeders should be placed less than three feet or more than ten feet from windows to prevent window strikes. Where squirrels are a problem, feeders and bird boxes should be more than 8 feet away from walls, trees and tall shrubs.

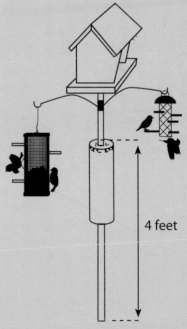

4 feet

Natural Foods

TOP LEFT   Non-native (and non-invasive) fruiting trees, such as this crabapple, may attract winter flocks of Pine Grosbeaks in some areas.

TOP RIGHT   Native trees like oaks provide natural food for many bird species, such as this Steller's Jay.

Keeping your bird feeder filled is a great way to see birds, but it is even better if you can complement your feeder with natural plants in your yard, patio or even balcony. North America has many different habitats and growing conditions, but here are some general rules to follow for any bird-loving garden plan.

Native vs. Ornamental

When given the choice, plant species that are native to your region. They will already be on a local bird's radar, so the birds will prefer them over non-native species. This is especially important when planting woody plants, such as trees, shrubs and vines.

You can also plant non-native ornamental plants, but it is very important that they are *not invasive*. Invasive species spread into natural habitats and have a very negative impact on the environment. Check with your local nature group or Audubon Society for a list of species that are good to plant in your area as well as a list of plants to avoid.

Local Seed Sources

When sourcing native plants, try to get your seedlings from nurseries that sell plants grown from local seed sources. This ensures that the plants you are investing in are adapted to your local growing conditions. For example, planting a Blue Ash seedling grown from a Tennessee seed source is not ideal if you live in northern Pennsylvania — the growing conditions are just too different.

Water Conservation

Planting species that you can grow on your site without needing "life support" helps conserve water. It is fine to have to water a new plant for the first season, but if it needs special watering for years, it is not an ideal choice. Know your site's moisture levels before buying your greenery: Is it muddy all year? Does it totally dry out in hot weather? Is it shady or sunny? How much rain do you get? Being able to answer these questions will help you purchase plants that will thrive.

Berries, Berries, Berries

Berries and other fruits are actually adapted to be eaten by birds — the birds end up dispersing the berries' seeds far and wide. Incorporating fruit-producing trees, shrubs and vines in your planting blueprints is an ideal way to attract more birds to your yard. Consider any native dogwoods, hollies, mountain ashes, serviceberries, blueberries, raspberries, crabapples, junipers, elderberries, hackberries, sumacs or cherries that are native to your area.

Bittersweet berries are highly prized by many birds, such as this Eastern Bluebird. Pictured here is Asian Bittersweet, which is very invasive in many areas. It isn't invasive where I live yet, but local gardeners are starting to plant the native bittersweet to replace these non-native plants (just in case).

ABOVE A Gray Catbird helps itself to a dogwood berry.

LEFT This native holly is called winterberry, and it likes to grow in wet conditions.

Don't Deadhead

Gardeners often deadhead their plants, meaning they pinch off any dead flower or seed heads to encourage new growth. However, leaving seed heads on your plants over the winter is a wonderful present to your local birds.

ABOVE LEFT   Annuals can attract many birds to your yard, especially large sunflowers. This Black-headed Grosbeak has hit the jackpot!

ABOVE RIGHT   Dry seed heads on perennials are especially attractive to finches, such as the American Goldfinch.

Grasses Are Important, Too!

Many small finches and sparrows get a lot of energy by eating grass and grain seeds. Try planting some noninvasive decorative grasses, but leave their seed heads on until the birdies have had their fill.

A male Indigo Bunting gorges on grass seeds.

ABOVE Orioles, like this Bullock's Oriole, like nectar, too! This one is foraging in a paloverde tree.

LEFT A wet spot near a stream or garden pond might support a hummingbird favorite: Cardinal Flower.

Be a Nectar Protector

Hummingbirds like to visit flowers as well as nectar feeders. Most hummers are especially attracted to red flowers, so be sure to incorporate them into your garden design. And remember that some woody plants also have red nectar-producing flowers. Consider Trumpet Creeper or Red Buckeye if they grow in your region. Everyone loves hummingbirds, so you may be able to get some advice from your local garden center on what works best in your area.

ABOVE LEFT   A male Baltimore Oriole puts its pointy beak to good use as it looks through some dead leaves for insect prey.

ABOVE RIGHT   Stealing from spiders: many birds, such as this male Rose-breasted Grosbeak, are known to steal insects out of spider webs.

BELOW   Earthworms are a favorite food of American Robins.

Insects and Other Invertebrates

Like them or not, insects really do run the world, at least the natural, terrestrial one. Over 96 percent of our small land birds feed insects and spiders to their young; even most of the seed-eating specialist birds do this. Insects provide important protein for the developing young, which need it for feather growth in particular.

Moth and butterfly caterpillars are crucial food sources. It is hard for some to think that caterpillars would be a desirable addition to your yard, but they are very important to the ecosystem, and the birds you attract will control the caterpillar numbers. To attract the most caterpillars, you should plant native trees and shrubs. Studies have shown that the following species support the greatest diversity of caterpillar species: oaks, willows, cherries, plums, birches, poplars, crabapples, maples, blueberries and cranberries. Oaks have been recorded as a food source for a whopping 534 moth and butterfly species!

A female Summer Tanager grabs a caterpillar.

BELOW Your backyard birds will help you protect your plants from insects, too. Here, a House Wren has caught a grasshopper and is bringing it to its nest to feed its young.

What's for Lunch?

Watching birds feeding their young at a nest is a great way to see what insects they are eating. This Great Crested Flycatcher has brought its young a caterpillar, dragonfly, grasshopper, butterfly, moth, fly, spider, snail and stink bug.

Water

Water is an important element in your wildlife garden, but offering it doesn't have to be complicated. A simple bird bath can attract many species of birds. The best baths are shallow; if they are too deep, small birds can't bathe in them. A water level of about ½ to 2 inches (1–5 cm) works for most backyard birds. You can provide different levels for different species by putting various flat rocks on the bottom of the bath.

It is important to change the water every few days or even daily if there are a lot of birds using your bird bath. Clean the bath every couple of weeks with a 10-percent bleach solution, and rinse the bath completely to get rid of any residual bleach before you refill it. Always wash your hands well afterward.

The more adventurous can design and install a pond or, better yet, a recirculating stream. Recirculating streams are particularly effective at attracting a wide variety of birds: the main part of the stream should be quite shallow, so birds can drink or bathe all along it. The sound of the moving water also helps attract birds. And because most birds are attracted to natural water features like streams and pond edges, you may get birds that normally don't come to your feeders, such as vireos and many warbler species.

A shallow recirculating stream is a great place where birds (such as this male Rose-breasted Grosbeak) can drink or bathe.

These American Robins are enjoying some water in a heated bird bath.

If a stream isn't suitable for your site, you can try to get a water jiggler, dripper or mister for your bird bath, to get the water moving and attract more birds. Hummingbirds like to fly through fine mist.

Water in Winter

So how do birds get water during the winter in colder climates? Many species eat snow, but there are also heated bird baths that can keep the water available for drinking and bathing year round, and these can be very popular with winter birds.

Safety First

If you have a bigger or deeper bath, especially one with steep sides, it is important to provide an escape route for recently fledged young birds or quail chicks so they don't drown. A slanted board or pile of stones will do the trick. If you have any rain barrels, make sure they have wire mesh covers to stop young birds from drowning in the deep water.

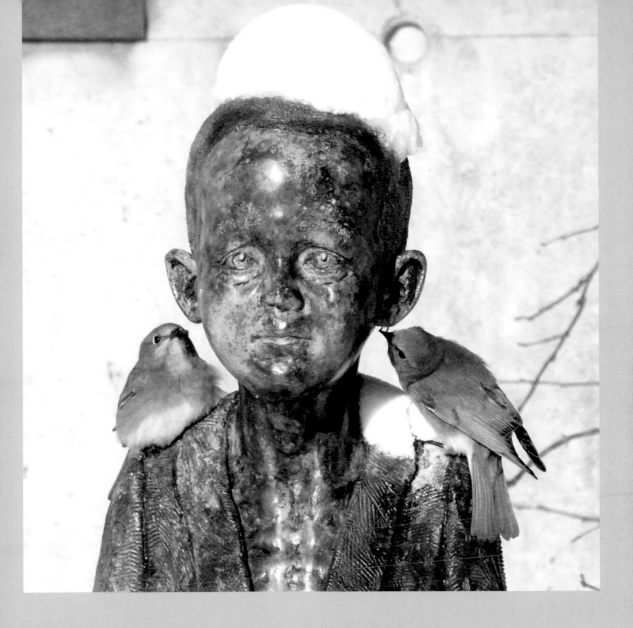

STORY TIME: Winter Water

Birds are attracted to the sound of moving or dripping water, especially during the winter. One very cold and windy morning in January, a flock of six Eastern Bluebirds showed up at a bittersweet vine outside of one of my workplace's buildings. Even though it was 14°F (–10°C), the vine was protected from the wind by a concrete wall, and the sun was beaming down on it.

Nearby, one of our statues, called *The Child*, had a large pile of snow on his head. As the sun warmed up the wall, the snow started to melt, flowing down the statue's head and dripping off his earlobes. The bluebirds noticed this, flew down and perched on the statue's shoulders so they could drink the drops as they fell, making the setting for a lovely photo. And the reflection of sunlight off the surrounding snow seemed to make the bluebirds an even brighter blue than normal.

Shelter

ABOVE LEFT I tied my old Christmas tree to my clothesline pole.

ABOVE RIGHT A Fox Sparrow shelters under the same tree during a severe ice storm.

Shelter is important for birds for many reasons. It can protect them from heavy rain, chilling winds, hot sun and aggressive rivals and predators. Shelter also provides crucial nesting sites, where brooding parents can hide with their eggs or young. In addition to cover-friendly plants, most backyards can easily provide other shelter sites.

Christmas Trees: Yuletide Hide

Getting rid of your Christmas tree in early January? Don't do it! You have an instant winter shelter for your birds if you just tie it to a post, clothesline or fence. It will provide a temporary but effective hiding spot. If you "steal" two more discarded Christmas trees from your neighbors' curbside after the holidays, you can tie the three of them together in a pyramid, creating a freestanding tree tepee.

Brush Piles

When your old Christmas tree turns brown and starts to lose its needles, you can put it in a back corner of your yard to create a pile of brush. Brush piles are favorite spots for species such as quail, sparrows, towhees, wrens and thrushes.

Wildlife Corridors

Planting a row of conifers or dense shrubs along one side of your yard gives visiting birds both an escape route and a wildlife highway. Lines of shrubs can help connect different backyards and give birds cover while they move from one area to another.

This Winter Wren (*left*) and Hermit Thrush (*bottom*) are frequent brush-pile users.

Nesting Material and Boxes

A female House Finch gets some dog hair that was stuffed into an empty suet feeder.

Having birds nest in your backyard is a true indication that you are doing something right! Don't just offer good nesting sites; offer nesting materials as well. Short bits of string, yarn and hair from your or your pet's hairbrush are all fair game. Don't include thread in this mix, though, because it is strong enough to entangle birds.

Nesting Boxes and Roosting Boxes

There are a few backyard birds known as "secondary cavity-nesters." These birds often use old woodpecker nests for their own nesting site. Woodpeckers (which are called primary cavity-nesters because they usually make their own nest holes) make specifically sized holes. Once the

ABOVE LEFT American Robins usually incorporate mud into their nests. Knowing what materials species use to build their nests can help you identify their nests in the winter, when they are more visible.

ABOVE RIGHT A House Finch collects some fluff for its nest lining.

LEFT This female Baltimore Oriole will use this piece of string in her bag-like nest.

Downy Woodpeckers provide homes for many secondary cavity-nesters.

woodpecker has finished nesting, the empty hole sometimes attracts a secondary cavity-nester that is appropriately sized for the hole.

Bird boxes are human-made cavities that many bird species use to raise their young or as shelter during bad weather.

You can build your own nest box or buy them premade. Because building a birdhouse is not complicated, making one of your own is a wonderful project to do with the children in your life, be they yours or nieces, nephews, grandkids, neighborhood youth or groups such as scouts and guides.

Instilling a sense of connectivity between kids and nature is every naturalist's responsibility. You can go from planning and designing the house to constructing and then installing it — and finally to observing a bird family using it!

Bird Box FAQs

How big should the hole be?
How big should the box be?

Because the requirements are different depending on where you live, asking a local expert is very helpful. Most Audubon societies and bluebird societies have plans you can use or a contact that will give you information. See the reference section on page 290 to find some great books on the subject, too.

Boxes for smaller birds, such as those listed below, should have a floor of about 4 to 6 square inches (25 to 40 cm²). Hole sizes are important because they can sometimes deter invasive species, such as House Sparrows and European Starlings.

Here is a quick reference chart for some common backyard birds that use nest boxes. If you are less choosy about which birds nest in your box, use a 1½-inch (3.8 cm) entrance hole; that way, most bird species can use the box. Always sand the hole so there are no rough edges inside or out.

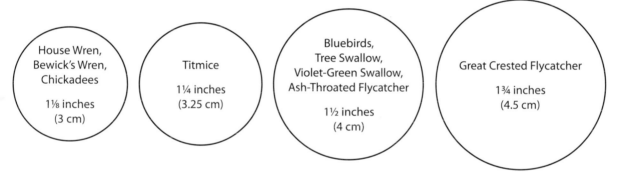

House Wren, Bewick's Wren, Chickadees

1⅛ inches (3 cm)

Titmice

1¼ inches (3.25 cm)

Bluebirds, Tree Swallow, Violet-Green Swallow, Ash-Throated Flycatcher

1½ inches (4 cm)

Great Crested Flycatcher

1¾ inches (4.5 cm)

American Robins, phoebes, House Finches and Carolina Wrens may use nest platforms placed under the eaves of your house.

Important!

Under the hole on the inside wall of the box, you need to either score or scratch the wood or add a bit of ¼ inch (0.5 cm) wire mesh. This works like a ladder and helps the adults and young climb out of the box — birds can sometimes get trapped in the box if the wood is too smooth. Sadly, bird watchers who forget this small but important detail risk opening their box and finding deceased birds inside.

What kind of wood should I use?
Should I paint it?

The best woods for bird boxes include pine, cedar and cypress. Exterior plywood is also fine, as long as it is not pressure-treated as the chemicals used are not good for nestlings. Purchase 1-inch-thick boards, which are actually closer to ¾ inch (2 cm) thick.

In most cases, boxes should be left unpainted to allow them to age and color naturally. In some areas, staining the exterior roof of the box to prevent rot and/or wear might be warranted.

Never paint or stain the inside of a bird box: the toxins are not good for the birds' health. When working with kids who may want to be a bit more creative, painting a few designs on the outside of the box with nontoxic paint is unlikely to harm or deter the birds.

There are many different styles of bird boxes. Ask your local Audubon Society or Nature Club for suggestions on the best plans for your area.

Decorative boxes such as this are attractive to birds but still need to follow the safety guidelines mentioned in this section. For example, boxes need to have a removable roof (as shown here) or side so old nests and mouse nests can be removed.

Where should I put the nest box?

The best place to put a nest box is on its own post with a baffle, away from where squirrels can jump to it (because they may chew the hole to make it bigger, so they can use the box themselves). If this isn't possible, you might need to attach a predator guard, depending on how many squirrels, cats or raccoons are in your area.

What is a predator guard?

It is a wire, wooden or plastic extension that's affixed around the hole of the box. It deters cats, raccoons and other unwanted guests, preventing them from reaching into the box and scooping out eggs or nestlings.

Do nest boxes need to be cleaned?
How often?

Every fall and again in late winter/very early spring, scrape out the box's contents, as mice will sometimes have moved in. Birds don't need last year's nest, and removing the old nests will reduce parasite numbers. Always wash your hands after cleaning out a nest box.

Squirrels and Cats

Squirrels

Squirrels are the most commonly complained-about "problem" of backyard bird feeders. Everyone has their own tolerance levels: I am fine with squirrels on the ground, but I don't like it when they are on my feeders because they often chew on them, damaging them in the process.

If possible, put your feeder on a pole at least 8 feet (2.5 m) away from tree branches and the sides of buildings, and add a baffle on the pole with the top at least 4 feet (1.25 m) above the ground. This will solve most squirrel-related problems. If your yard can't accommodate that design, invest in a good squirrel-proof feeder.

It can be very fun to watch these clever rodents try to figure out how to get to the food! Enjoy their antics, and do some mammal-watching along with your bird-watching.

Hanging your feeder from a wire or clothesline is not a good strategy.

OPPOSITE, TOP LEFT Squirrels are built for climbing, so it's no surprise that they are good at getting into feeders.

OPPOSITE, TOP RIGHT Not all squirrel-proof feeders live up to their name.

OPPOSITE Squirrels can throw their weight around and evict most birds from a choice feeding spot.

My favorite squirrel-proof feeder proves to be too complicated for yet another uninvited dinner guest. It works because the weight of the squirrel closes the ports. You can adjust the spring inside so that it can deter squirrels only or squirrels and large birds as well (but see page 262 to discover how a smart grackle worked its way around it).

RIGHT   A good baffle is an important piece of bird-feeding equipment.

Papa's Do-It-Yourself Squirrel Baffle

My dad made a squirrel baffle out of easy-to-obtain materials that kept his feeder free of squirrels for years.

Materials

24-inch (61 cm) length of stovepipe, 6–8 inches (15–20 cm) wide

A short length of 2" x 8" lumber

Nails or screws

A clamp that will fit your feeder pole

Cut a circle in the wood with a diameter of 6–8 inches (15–20 cm).

Cut a hole in the middle of that circle that is ½ inch (1.25 cm) wider than the diameter of your feeder pole.

Insert the circle of wood into one end of the stovepipe (like a plug), and, using the nails or screws, attach it through the pipe and into the sides of the piece of wood.

Remove the feeder from your feeder pole.

Put the clamp on the feeder pole at least 4 feet (1.25 m) above ground level.

Place the baffle onto the pole so that it is resting on the clamp. You want the baffle to be able to move, so it is only resting on the clamp, not firmly attached to it.

Place the feeder back at the top of the pole.

Now watch confused squirrels try to get to your feeder. This baffle is long enough to deter raccoons as well — hopefully.

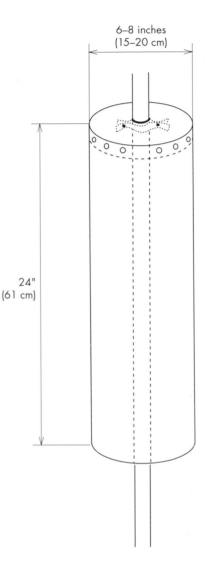

6–8 inches
(15–20 cm)

24"
(61 cm)

This feeder is unlikely to attract any birds!

ABOVE RIGHT Even many well-fed cats hunt.

Cats

Outdoor cats are bad news for birds and other wildlife. Even well-fed cats may hunt, and because there are millions of cats in North America, their collective predatory behavior is devastating bird populations.

The easiest solution is for all cat owners to just keep their cats inside. This can be challenging if the cat already goes outside, but there are helpful tips at catsandbirds.ca and abcbirds.org/program/cats-indoors. You can also contact your local ASPCA or Humane Society. Other solutions include outdoor enclosures, often called catios, that allow cats to spend time outside while keeping them safe from predators — and keeping animals they may want to prey on safe from them.

A bird feeder can be a great thing for an indoor cat. My indoor-only cats spend hours watching my feeders — it's like kitty television. But since you can't control every cat in your neighborhood, there are ways to reduce the chances of them catching your feeder birds.

No Place to Hide

Cats can ambush birds by hiding in one spot until the bird gets close enough. If you make sure you don't have any bushes or tall perennials near your feeder, you reduce a cat's chances of surprising the birds.

The Jump-the-Fence Defense

Installing a low wire mesh fence (it only needs to be a couple of feet high) around the outside edge of your feeder area can help protect your birds. Because a stalking cat will have to jump over the fence to grab any ground-feeding birds, the birds have a chance to see the oncoming predator and escape.

I put up this temporary fence recently when a new cat started showing up in my yard. It gives the birds an extra moment to escape.

LEFT   An outdoor "catio" keeps your cat safe from predators and cars while protecting your backyard birds.

RIGHT   Indoor cats can enjoy the birds, too!

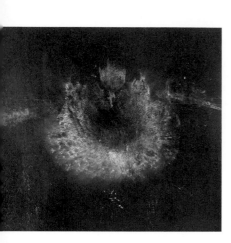

Windows

This is the imprint left by a Mourning Dove after it hit a window.

ABOVE RIGHT This Red-bellied Woodpecker tried to fly through a window and was killed. If you find a bird that has survived a window strike but is not flying away, put it in a paper bag in a quiet and safe place for an hour or two (make sure the bag is securely clipped shut but still has an air opening). Then try to release the bird outside by gently sliding it out of the bag. Sometimes birds are only stunned and can recover, though some of these birds may succumb to their injuries later.

Watching your birds in your backyard or on your patio is what makes bird-feeding fun. Unfortunately, the windows or sliding glass doors we watch through are a potential hazard for the birds. But there are solutions. It is important to know that the main reason birds hit house windows is because they see the outside reflection and think they can fly through it. This is why anything put on the inside of a window is likely to fail: the problem is the outside of the window. Also, a couple of hawk silhouettes stuck on the outside of a window will only stop the birds where the silhouettes are located.

The best solution is to cover the outside of the window with something that allows you to see out but also allows birds to see that the window is a barrier. I've used window markers (yup, those washable ones that kids use to draw on windows) on the outside of my problem windows to great effect. I just draw little snowflakes or Ms (like those flying seagulls you drew as a kid) about 2 inches (5 cm) apart on the window.

Unfortunately, every time the window gets rained on, the marks wash off. In rainy climates, your best bet is to apply commercially made sticker "dots" that help the birds see that the window is a barrier. These work wonderfully, and you don't even notice them after a couple of days. Try www.featherfriendly.com or www.flap.org for more information.

ABOVE This photo shows the dots I applied to the outside of my back sliding glass door. These dots stop the birds from thinking they can fly to the reflected trees.

LEFT From the inside, the dots blend into the background and don't distract from watching the birds at the feeders.

This Northern Cardinal is in full attack mode against itself. It likely won't get hurt but may spend a lot of time trying to evict the reflected "intruder." If possible, try to cover the outside of the problem section during the breeding season.

3
Bird Feeder Building Plans

Hopper Feeder

This feeder is worth the extra effort needed to build it. Birds of all sizes will use it; it is easy to fill and keeps a large amount of feed dry.

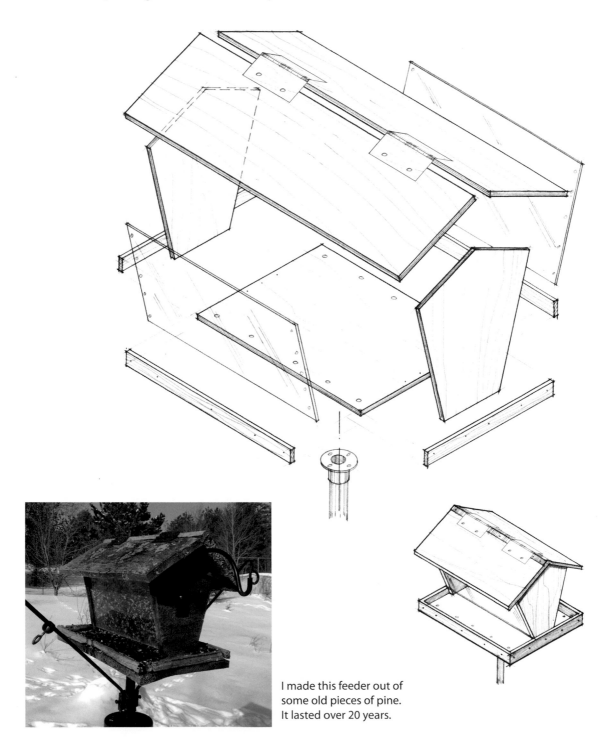

I made this feeder out of some old pieces of pine. It lasted over 20 years.

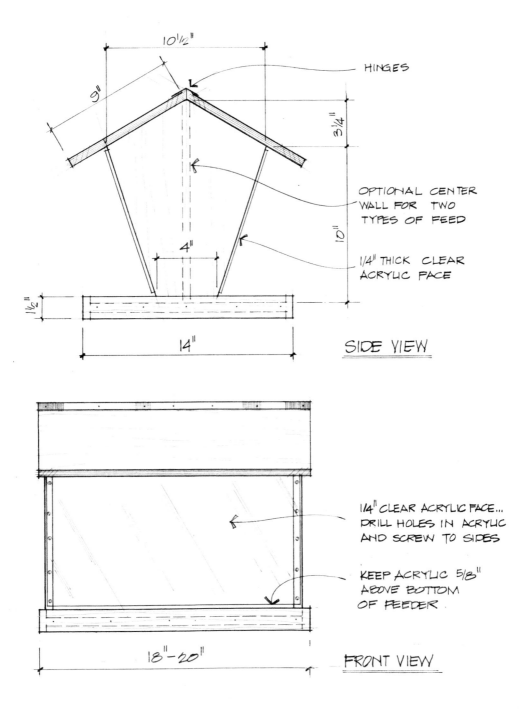

10½"

9"

HINGES

3¼"

OPTIONAL CENTER WALL FOR TWO TYPES OF FEED

10"

¼" THICK CLEAR ACRYLIC FACE

4"

1½"

14"

SIDE VIEW

¼" CLEAR ACRYLIC FACE... DRILL HOLES IN ACRYLIC AND SCREW TO SIDES

KEEP ACRYLIC 5/8" ABOVE BOTTOM OF FEEDER

18"-20"

FRONT VIEW

Roofed Platform Feeder

This feeder will keep the snow and rain off of your seeds and your birds. It will also provide shade in hot, sunny climates and, if oriented correctly, block wind on blustery days.

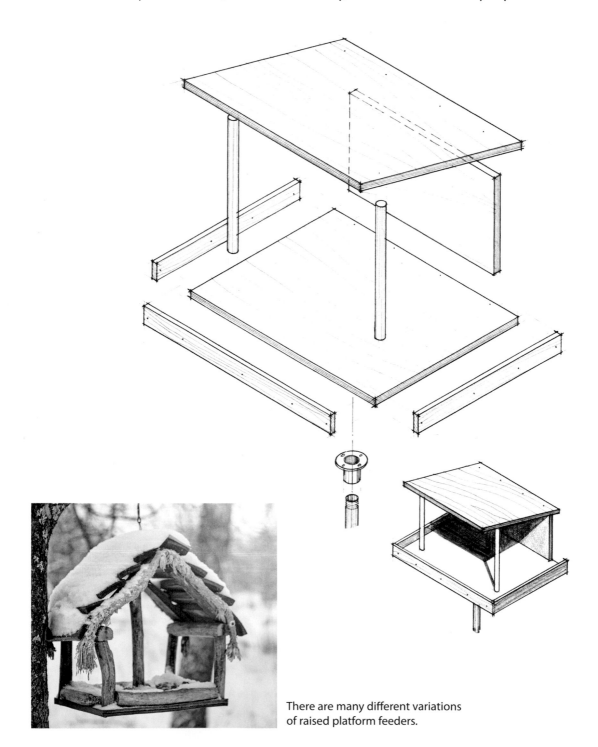

There are many different variations of raised platform feeders.

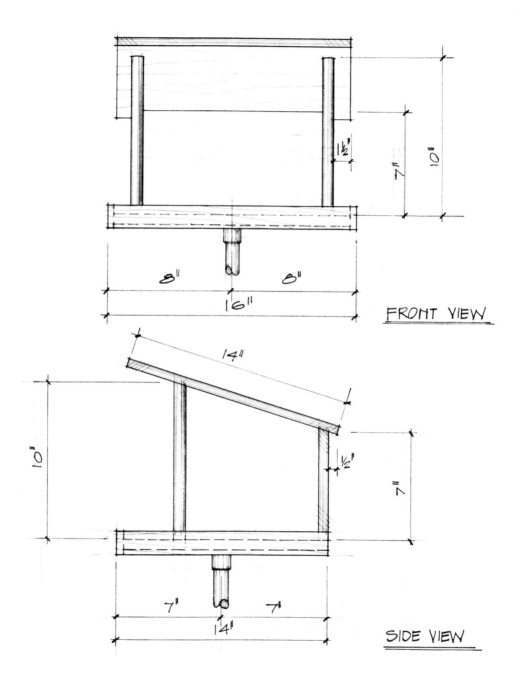

1½"

7"

10"

8"

8"

16"

FRONT VIEW

14"

10"

½"

7"

7"

7"

14"

SIDE VIEW

Raised Platform Feeder

Keeping seed off the ground will stop the feeder from getting wet and going moldy. Many individual birds can fit on the feeder, but it may not be a good choice if there are a lot of squirrels.

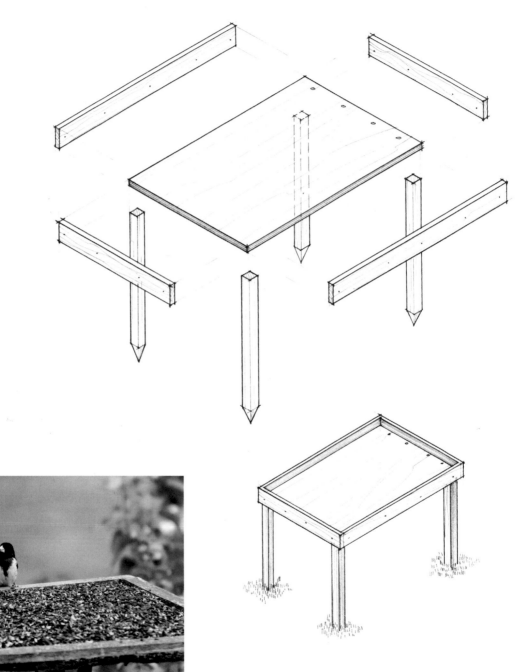

Table feeders can be mounted in a variety of ways.

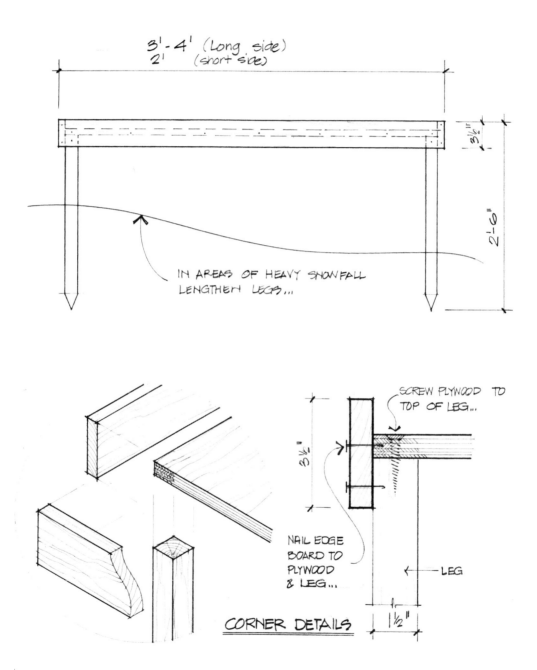

3'- 4' (Long side)
2' (short side)

3½"

2'-6"

IN AREAS OF HEAVY SNOWFALL
LENGTHEN LEGS...

SCREW PLYWOOD TO
TOP OF LEG...

3½"

NAIL EDGE
BOARD TO
PLYWOOD
& LEG...

LEG

1½"

CORNER DETAILS

Window Shelf Feeder

It may seem strange, but having feeders really close to windows may be safer for birds because if they are frightened, they can't get up enough speed to hurt themselves if they hit the window. Window feeders are also a great way to see your backyard visitors.

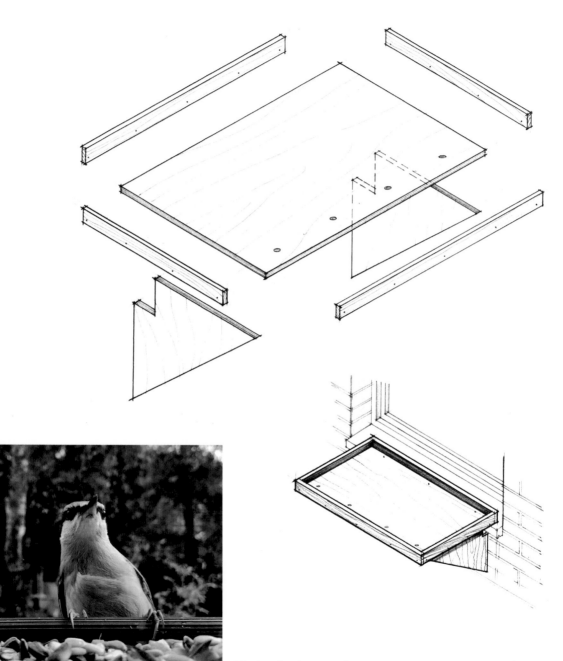

Window feeders can give you a very close look at your feeder birds!

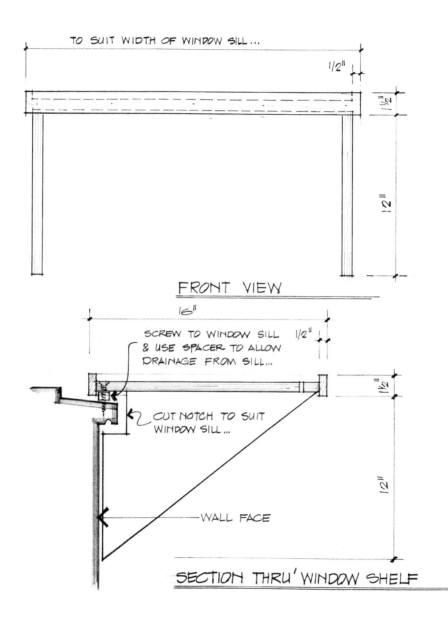

TO SUIT WIDTH OF WINDOW SILL...

1/2"

1 1/2"

12"

FRONT VIEW

16"

SCREW TO WINDOW SILL
& USE SPACER TO ALLOW
DRAINAGE FROM SILL...

1/2"

1 1/2"

CUT NOTCH TO SUIT
WINDOW SILL...

12"

WALL FACE

SECTION THRU' WINDOW SHELF

4

Bird Behavior
and Biology

STORY TIME:
Sparrows vs. Robin

One summer my backyard lawn was infested with grubs, which caused the grass to wither and die. My local male American Robin took advantage of this and dug holes with his beak until he flipped a grub out.

After a few days of watching him do this, I noticed some House Sparrows had showed up. They hopped around the robin as he dug and grabbed the grub when the robin flung it out, before he could turn around and get it himself. Smart sparrows.

A day later, the robin began to dig a hole, but as he got close to where the grub was, he stopped. He waited until the sparrows lost interest, and only after they left did he quickly continue and get to the grub. Smart robin.

But the story continued. As the robin was digging a hole a couple of days later, the house sparrows started flying back and forth a few feet over his head. The robin continued to dig because the sparrows weren't hopping around him. When he flung the grub out of the ground, the sparrows swooped down from the air and grabbed it before the robin could. Smarter sparrows.

A Black-capped Chickadee gets oil from its preen gland during a preening session.

After a few days of cloudy weather, the sun finally popped out. This female Northern Cardinal stopped mid-chew and assumed a stationary sunning position while still holding the seed in her beak!

Bird Behavior

Identifying birds is a fun activity, sort of like a scavenger hunt that you can do anywhere. But don't forget to really watch the birds. They have complex behaviors that help them survive, and your backyard is the perfect place to take everything in. Each bird species in the identification section (which starts on page 128) has a biological tidbit, and many of these are behaviors you can watch for.

Here is a list of some general behaviors that are happening near your feeder.

When water isn't available, many species, such as this Scaled Quail, use sand or dust for bathing.

A Scarlet Tanager has a bath. Birds' feathers are often so waterproof that the bathers have to work hard to get themselves wet!

Feather Maintenance

Feather aren't just for flight. They allow birds to stay warm, stay dry, attract a mate and communicate. Because they are so important, birds take time to preen their feathers with their beak. This keeps their feathers in tip-top shape and free of parasites. The birds also have a preen, or uropygial, gland on their lower back, which provides oil to help keep

FAR LEFT A White-breasted Nuthatch uses this crack in a four-by-four post on my back deck to hold a sunflower seed still so it can peck it open. Red-breasted Nuthatches and Downy Woodpeckers also use this crack to open seeds.

LEFT This White-breasted Nuthatch is a kleptoparasite, meaning it is stealing food from another bird. In this case, it is taking an acorn from the storage larder of an Acorn Woodpecker.

their feathers waterproof. Other feather maintenance behaviors incorporate water, snow or dust bathing, sunning (see page 203) and anting (see page 196).

Feeding

Birds have different feeding behaviors, which allow them to get nourishment that might otherwise be unavailable.

An American Robin in this position only means one thing — there is a worm underfoot! And sure enough, he dove into the dirt and pulled one up. See if you can tell when a robin is about to pounce.

This Anna's Hummingbird is flaring its throat feathers in an attempt to intimidate a rival male.

This Downy Woodpecker is assuming a threat posture and directing its aggression at another of its own species.

Threat Displays

A threat display is a way for an animal to show a potential rival its mood or intentions; think of a dog lowering its head and raising the fur on its neck and shoulders. The function of these displays is to stop an actual physical interaction: fights can lead to injuries, and injuries can threaten an animal's survival. Most animals size each other up during aggressive interactions first, so they can decide if an actual physical confrontation is needed.

For many birds, especially males, a lot of aggression happens during the formation and defense of breeding territories. A male defends his territory because his space must provide food for not only himself, but for his mate and his growing young as well. Sharing food sources with others of his species is not an option if he wants to succeed. There is still aggression during the nonbreeding season, but many birds flock together and are more tolerant of each other.

Open beak threats, raised crests and spread wings and tails are signaling aggression between these two Blue Jays.

Aggression Within the Same Species

When a threat display doesn't deter one or both of the challengers, a fight may result. Small birds fight with their beaks and feet and may hit each other with their wings. Larger birds have a variety of fighting techniques. For example, raptors may grapple in the air with their claws together.

Aggression Between Different Species

Birds compete with other bird species for food. They also compete for resources such as water and nesting sites. Some aggression may also be seen between birds and nonavian species.

TOP These Horned Larks are fighting over a feeding spot in their winter territory. These fights become more and more common as spring approaches.

ABOVE LEFT Here, a pair of mockingbirds fight off an intruder in their breeding territory.

ABOVE RIGHT These American Robins are fighting over a bit of snowless feeding habitat during their migration.

ABOVE   Jays are often the most dominant birds at a feeder, but here a Red-bellied Woodpecker wins a battle with a Blue Jay. The jay is trying to make itself bigger, with its raised wing display and raised crest, and is jumping away because it is being threatened by the open beak display of the woodpecker.

LEFT   A resident Black-capped Chickadee is defending its suet from a newly arrived migrant Pine Warbler. Both birds are using open beak threats.

Bird Behavior and Biology   **97**

ABOVE   Here is an example of interspecies (i.e., between two different species) aggression for a non-food resource. An American Robin uses its size and open beak threat to force a Cedar Waxwing to give up its bathing spot.

RIGHT   A Mourning Dove defends its feeding spot from a chipmunk with a raised wing and tail spread display.

Courtship

Once a male holds a territory, the next part of a bird's breeding cycle is attracting and bonding with a mate. Many species accomplish this through different displays. These actions strengthen the bonding process; the pair will need to be a good team to be able to defend their territory, nest and care for their nestlings and fledglings.

During courtship, nest-building and incubation, the male may be seen feeding the female. This likely strengthens their pair-bond and gives the female the extra energy she needs to produce and warm her eggs.

A male Northern Cardinal courtship-feeding a female.

Nestling Care

If you are lucky enough to have birds nest near your home, you may be able to watch the parents brooding and feeding their young. You can watch to see what food items the adults are bringing in and see the young become more and more demanding for food as they get bigger.

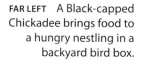

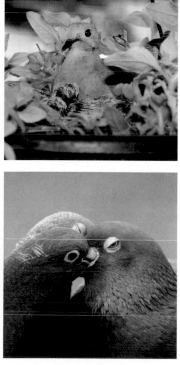

FAR LEFT A Black-capped Chickadee brings food to a hungry nestling in a backyard bird box.

LEFT TOP A Mourning Dove is nesting in a hanging basket, giving us front-row seats for watching the family grow.

LEFT BOTTOM Instead of bringing their young seeds or insects, pigeons feed them "pigeon milk," a substance they produce in their crop.

Fledgling Care

A male Eastern Bluebird is very busy feeding mealworms to his four fledglings.

Believe it or not, the real work for the parents begins after the young leave the nest! Many species take care of their young longer out of the nest than in it. Fledglings (young that have left the nest) can take a long time to learn how to feed themselves on their own, so the parents keep feeding them for weeks. You may see Mom and Dad bring their fledglings to your feeders.

RIGHT A female House Finch has brought one of her fledglings to a sunflower feeder.

OPPOSITE A female Downy Woodpecker feeds a fledgling a shelled sunflower seed.

from a tree to escape, so it just flattened itself as low as it could and stayed still. I scanned the skies for the Red-tail but couldn't see it.

After a few seconds, the hawk still hadn't appeared. The squirrel began to relax and resumed its nest search. Then I heard an oriole call — but it came from the starling. Then there was a loud Red-tail scream again — it was also the starling!

The squirrel reacted again, looking left and right and up and down; it couldn't tell where the "hawk" was. Now the starling just repeated the Red-tailed call, not the garbled or oriole calls. The squirrel slowly edged to the far side of the roof and then jumped to a nearby tree and took off.

The starling had saved its nest by making a Red-tail call! The jury is still out on how much the starling understood about what it had done, but it had tried three different calls and then repeated the one that caused the squirrel to react.

Another day, I was at home, in my driveway, getting something out of the back of my station wagon. I heard a sound coming from the side of my house, so I turned to see what it was. A starling came flying around the corner with a Sharp-shinned Hawk hot on its tail. It looked like the starling was toast.

While it could have flown in any direction, the starling flew directly at me.

It hit my side and ricocheted into my car. The Sharp-shinned Hawk then almost hit me, too, but it swerved at the last minute so only its wing tip brushed me. The hawk continued on its way, leaving the starling and I trying to catch our breath. The starling's maneuver saved its life and required some quick thinking. It sat on one of the headrests for a minute, panting, and then took off, leaving me very impressed with its successful escape.

STORY TIME:
The Brainy European Starling

European Starlings aren't going to win a popularity contest, but they can be fun to watch. A pair of starlings once nested in the eaves of the nature center where I work. One day, I saw a gray squirrel on the roof, sniffing around close to the entrance of the starling nest. Uh oh, I thought, that squirrel may be after the starlings' eggs. One of the parent starlings was perched nearby and was clearly upset by the presence of the squirrel. The starling made some garbled noises at the squirrel, but it didn't deter the squirrel.

Suddenly there was the whistling scream of a Red-tailed Hawk. The squirrel panicked instantly. It was completely exposed on the roof and too far

This is my favorite peanut feeder because the jays feeding at it have to figure out a few things. When the feeder is full, getting the upper peanuts out is easy, but as the feeder empties, it gets harder. The Blue Jay on the left tried repeatedly to pull a peanut up out of the coil, but the wires were too close together and it failed. The next Blue Jay landed on the feeder, hung upside down and deftly pulled a peanut out of the bottom, where the wires are farther apart. Genius!

Bird Intelligence

While some might think being called a "bird brain" is an insult, I consider it a compliment! Birds' brains are structured differently than mammalian brains, but they are no less complex. While comparing intelligence between species is very difficult, some studies show that birds such as ravens, crows and jays have intelligence levels similar to primates.

Recognizing Individual Birds

A Black-capped Chickadee with an injured leg visits my feeder. It was an infrequent visitor, so I was pretty sure it wasn't a member of my regular chickadee flock.

Scientists study individual birds by adding colored bands to their legs. Each one is a different color combination (see page 171). Since you can't do that, this section outlines a few ways to recognize certain individual birds.

Being able to identify an individual bird is a wonderful way to connect with our feathered friends. Recent scientific studies have proven that many animals have individual personalities, so recognizing a specific individual is a great

This Song Sparrow had a stress molt. This occurs when a predator grabs the tail of a bird and all of the prey's tail feathers fall out instantly. This is a survival adaptation: not having a tail is better than dying. This is a temporary individual ID feature — the feathers will eventually grow back.

Feather changes can sometimes be temporary identification clues. The House Finch on the top has recently left its nest and still has some nestling down on its head. The House Finch in the middle is a young male that is molting into his first adult plumage. Both of these characteristics will be lost or change in only a few days.

BOTTOM   Usually, damaged feathers don't work well to identify individuals because they often fall out or are removed within a few days. This female cardinal, however, had a damaged secondary feather that stuck upright when she perched, and it lasted the whole winter, before it fell out in the spring.

This Eastern Towhee has a left wing droop. He could still fly, but he may have had trouble migrating south, as he stayed much farther north over the winter than this species normally does. We named him "Joey the Snowy Towhee."

Some species, such as Evening Grosbeaks, have colored markings that vary slightly in shape. Can you see the difference between the yellow eyebrows of these four males? It is important to note that these shapes can change depending on the mood of the bird.

This perched Black-billed Magpie only has one leg. How does that affect its behavior and ability to survive? Here, it loses its perch to one of its flock-mates.

way to learn about birds' behavior. Does "Leftie" always approach the feeder from the same side? Is she dominant over others of her species? What times of day does she visit? Is she alone or with others? What foods does she prefer? The questions are endless! Plus, it is just nice to see a specific bird returning and know that "Leftie" is still around.

What Is Wrong with That Bird?

The beak on this Red-winged Blackbird has obvious deformities.

Sometimes a bird will visit your feeder with some kind of anomaly that makes it stand out. Here are some examples of some strange looking birds.

Beak Deformities

Sometimes birds can injure their beak or it does not grow properly. Many birds can survive with this problem, but it likely makes survival much more difficult. There is a website

A Mountain Chickadee with an awkwardly growing beak.

ABOVE   The upper mandible of this American Robin is bent. Eating berries and crabapples wasn't a problem, but it likely had more difficulties collecting insects and earthworms.

RIGHT   This European Starling's lower mandible kept growing past the tip of its upper mandible.

that collects information on birds with deformed beaks: alaska.usgs.gov/science/biology/landbirds/beak_deformity/index.html

Bald Birds

Most birds molt their feathers gradually so they always have protection from cold and weather. Sometimes, however, they may lose all of their head feathers at once, as seen on the Northern Cardinal at right. But don't worry — they will grow back! Loss of feathers can sometimes be a sign of parasites or a nutritional deficiency; these birds may also show unhealthy-looking skin.

What's with the White?

Some individual birds may have odd, pale coloration, white patches or even be all white. These conditions are related to pigment-production problems. They are a great benefit to human observers, as we can use them to recognize individuals. However, they are not a benefit to the bird. Depending on the extent of the loss of pigment, it may be extra challenging for the bird to avoid predators, find a mate or even have strong enough feathers to survive. In the case of albino birds, which have pink eyes, the condition affects their vision and most don't make it to adulthood.

Can you recognize the Ruby-throated Hummingbird, Dark-eyed Junco, American Robin and European Starling shown here?

Sharp-shinned Hawks are native hunters that might visit your backyard.

Nature's Predators

While house cats are not a natural part of your backyard ecosystem, there are lots of predators that are. For example, many species of hawk will try to catch the birds at your feeder. I am always excited when I see a hawk zip through my yard: Will it be successful? Did the vigilant Blue Jays warn everyone in time? Can I tell what species of hawk it is? By providing shelter, such as conifers or dense shrubs, you will give your feeder birds a chance to escape, but remember that some will be caught. This is all a part of natural food webs and represents a healthy ecosystem. See pages 285–289 for some examples of raptors that may visit your yard.

BELOW LEFT Most birds are predators themselves, at least for some of the year. Here, a House Wren has caught a praying mantis.

BELOW RIGHT The prey becomes the predator: Praying mantises sometimes catch and kill hummingbirds.

LEFT The southwest has its own special predator: the Greater Roadrunner. This bird has been known to catch and eat small backyard birds.

The Cooper's Hawk: Coming to a Bird Feeder Near You!

Common over much of North America, Cooper's Hawks are avian predators extraordinaire. Their speedy flight and maneuverability make them especially efficient bird catchers. They seem to especially like pigeons and doves, and it is possible that, historically, one of their main prey species was the now-extinct Passenger Pigeon.

Seeing a natural predator like a Cooper's Hawk in action is a thrilling part of having a bird feeder.

STORY TIME: Ronnie the Cooper's Hawk

I often have a few Cooper's Hawks and Sharp-shinned Hawks patrolling my feeder area each winter. Last year, I had one very large adult female Cooper's Hawk that visited my yard consistently. Her deep red eyes, orange-barred breast and gray upperparts showed that she was an adult. My daughter named her Ronnie, and we saw a lot of her.

One day, I saw her chasing a Mourning Dove across the yard. Just when it seemed to be curtains for the dove, Ronnie only grabbed the dove's tail, pulling out most of the feathers. She had missed! What a lucky dove.

A couple of days later, I saw Ronnie chasing another dove, and the same thing happened — she grabbed at the dove but only got feathers.

The third time I saw this happen, I started to wonder what was going on. Predators miss far more than they succeed, but Ronnie seemed very well fed, and our dove numbers were definitely dropping. Then I noticed that the tailless Mourning Doves that had escaped her were only at the feeders for a day or two before they disappeared.

It is always hard to know exactly what is happening in this type of situation, but could Ronnie have just been "damaging" the doves on purpose so that they were easier to catch later, when she was actually hungry? A tailless Mourning Dove would likely have a harder time escaping.

I'll probably never know the real answer to this question, but as more and more studies show the complexity of animal intelligence, it's certainly possible that Ronnie was planning ahead.

Predator Detectors

Woodpeckers

Woodpeckers are the best at signaling the location of a perched hawk in your yard. While other birds usually take off at once, woodpeckers often jump to one side of the feeder or tree trunk. They will then keep the feeder or tree trunk between them and the predator. If the predator moves from the left side of your yard to the right side, the woodpeckers will scooch from the right side to the left side of their tree trunk. This not only lets you know a predator is there, but it will give you a direction to look in!

These two Downy Woodpeckers gave away the position of a perched Cooper's Hawk in my yard. The birds kept still on the post and feeder, using them to hide themselves from the raptor.

Mobbers

Mobbing is a great behavior to watch for. Smaller birds often scream at a predator to drive it away. Though smaller than the predator, these birds are usually pretty safe since they've discovered the predator and it no longer has the element of surprise.

However, the small birds must still watch the predator carefully, and that will impede their regular foraging duties. Ideally, they don't want a predator there at all. By mobbing it, the small birds may be able to drive it off. During the breeding season, some small birds will fly at and even peck hawks to get them away from their nesting area.

CENTER Red-winged Blackbird is chasing a Red-shouldered Hawk from its territory.

BOTTOM A Black-capped Chickadee reveals the presence of a Long-eared Owl.

The specially arranged toes
of woodpeckers, such as this
Red-headed Woodpecker, help
them cling to vertical tree trunks
and branches.

Adaptations

Birds have adapted to live in their special spot or "niche" in the ecosystem. Their bodies show this by having unique shapes; these adaptations help them survive.

LEFT This Black-headed Grosbeak's large beak allows it to crack open even the toughest seeds.

BELOW The short, round wings of this Ring-necked Pheasant allow her to have a sudden burst of speed to get away from predators.

Beak Shapes

Beaks are a bird's hands. They use their beak to manipulate food, preen their feathers and build their nests. There is a great variety of beak shapes, each relating to the bird's particular needs and environment.

The Knife: Shrike
Also known as the Butcherbird, the shrike's beak is sharp enough to kill and cut up prey.

The Tweezers: Creeper
The thin, curved beak of the Brown Creeper helps it find insects and spiders in cracks in bark.

The Probe: Starling
Starlings can often be seen sticking their beak into the soil and then spreading it open to find insects.

The Pick: Woodpecker
The woodpecker's extremely strong beak can take chunks out of tree trunks to get at the insects inside.

The Nutcracker: Grosbeak
The strong beak of the grosbeak can crack large seeds like cherry stones.

The Syringe: Hummingbird
This needle-like beak allows the hummer to get to the nectar inside flowers so it can pump it up with its tongue.

The Straw: Dove
Pigeons and doves are the only birds in your backyard that can suck up water with their beak. Other birds have to dip their beak into the water and then tilt their head back.

The Pincher: Warbler
The warbler's beak allows these mainly insectivorous birds to grab insects off of leaves, buds, twigs and branches.

The Tongs: Phoebe
Flycatchers like the phoebe have flattened beaks to help them catch flying insects.

The Retractor: Crossbill
The crossbill uses its crazy beak to spread open the scales on pine cones so that it can reach the seeds with its tongue.

The Pry Bar: Nuthatch
Nuthatches use their beak to pry into cracks in trees and chip off bark to find hidden insects.

The Swiss Army Knife: Crow
Crows have a versatile beak that suits their varied omnivorous diet.

Foot Shapes

Most birds have four toes: three in the front and one at the back. This common arrangement works well for preening and perching in most situations. Some species, however, have special feet for special reasons.

Spurs: Ring-necked Pheasant
Many chicken-like birds have spurs on their legs. They use these when fighting during courtship and territorial battles.

Snowshoes: Ruffed Grouse
In autumn, these hardy birds grow pectinations on the sides of their toes. Pectinations are tiny projections with a comb-like structure that increases the surface area of the grouse's feet, which allows it to walk more easily on top of the snow. The pectinations disappear in the spring.

Grappling Hooks: Cooper's Hawk
The Cooper's Hawk uses its long, curved claws and strong toes to grab prey, kill it and hold it in place while it dismembers and eats it.

Zygodactyl Feet: Red-bellied Woodpecker
This is a fun word for feet that have two toes pointing forward and two pointing backward. A woodpecker's zygodactyl feet combine with its stiff tail to create a tripod of strength, helping the bird brace itself as it hammers for insects hidden in and on tree trunks.

Tiny Feet: Ruby-throated Hummingbird
When you fly like an insect and never need to walk, feet don't need to be big or complex. Hummingbirds have tiny feet, just big enough for landing and a bit of preening.

Straight Hind Claw: Horned Lark
Most small birds are good at perching because they spend a lot of time in trees, shrubs, herbaceous plants and grasses. But some, like larks and longspurs, spend most of their time on the ground. These birds have straight hind claws that help them easily walk on flat surfaces.

Wing Shapes

All of our backyard birds can fly, but some have special adaptations for specific flight techniques.

Hovering: Anna's Hummingbird
No other bird can control its flight as well as the hummingbird. When a bird pumps its wing forward, it creates lift and thrust. Unlike other birds, hummingbirds can pump their wings forward and backward, allowing them to hover in one spot and even fly backward.

Soaring: Common Raven
Common Ravens use their long, wide wings to catch warm air currents and other upwellings of air. This allows them to travel great distance with barely a flap.

Speeding: Rock Pigeon
The long, pointed wings of the Rock Pigeon allow it to fly very quickly. Speeds of up to 90 miles per hour (145 km/h) have been recorded.

Sprinting: Ring-necked Pheasant
When it needs to escape predators, the ground-dwelling Ring-necked Pheasant jumps into the air with strong, fast flaps of its short wings. It can attain flight speeds of 38 miles per hour (61 km/h) relatively quickly. However, the power doesn't last long, and in most cases pheasants fly less than 650 feet (200 m) before landing.

Maneuvering: Sharp-shinned Hawk
The Sharp-shinned Hawk puts its short, round wings to a different use. They allow this predatory bird to do quick turns and move through forested areas while chasing smaller birds.

Bird
Identification

Can you see how the chickadee is not much smaller than this woodpecker? That can help you identify the woodpecker as a Downy and not a similar-looking, but larger, Hairy Woodpecker.

ONE OF THE BEST things about having a bird feeder or a naturalized backyard is that you never know what species may show up. Some, like the Rose-breasted Grosbeak or Steller's Jay, are easy to identify, but others can be very challenging. The first rule of bird identification is to be able to say "I don't know."

Really, it's okay to say it! Identifying birds takes practice, and the amount of information you need to learn can be daunting, so it is important to be able to admit defeat and just enjoy looking at a bird! The next time you see it, you may notice a field mark that you didn't before and that might lead you to a correct identification.

The birds in this book were chosen by exploring information on the Project Feederwatch website and seeing what species have been recorded during backyard feeder surveys. So, most of these birds can be attracted to a feeder. Other species that may not be attracted to feeders are in your area, too, so you may need a more comprehensive bird field guide for some identifications.

Species	Length
Ruby-throated Hummingbird and Black-chinned Hummingbird	3¾ inches (9.5 cm)
Black-capped Chickadee	5 inches (13 cm)
Dark-eyed Junco	6¼ inches (16 cm)
Downy Woodpecker	6¾ inches (17 cm)
Brown-headed Cowbird	7½ inches (19 cm)
Red-winged Blackbird	8¾ inches (22 cm)
American Robin	10 inches (25.5 cm)
Blue Jay and Steller's Jay	11 inches (28 cm)
Rock Pigeon	12½ inches (32 cm)
American Crow	17½ inches (45.5 cm)
Red-tailed Hawk	19 inches (48 cm)

Size

Determining size can be tough. A bird on a leafless branch often looks way bigger than one hidden in a leafy bush. But if the bird is visiting your feeder, you might be able to tell how big it is compared to other common backyard birds that you have already identified. I compare the length of each bird identified in this book to a common species found across North America (see above chart for actual measurements).

Remember that tail length, beak length and body shape between species can be very different, so overall length can be a bit misleading: a Steller's Jay is longer than a Gambel's Quail but weighs half as much.

Shape

While field marks are often more distinctive for beginners, eventually you will get used to a bird's shape and that will help you identify it. This can be hard at first so try comparing the shapes of easy-to-identify birds to get used to it. Then try to compare the shapes of unfamiliar birds. Ask yourself the following questions:

What is the beak shape?
Is it long? Is it short? Is it curved? Is it pointy?

It is obvious that a Downy Woodpecker (right) is much smaller than a Hairy Woodpecker (left) when they are side by side, but when they are viewed separately, it can be much more difficult to tell them apart. But can you see the difference between their head shapes and beak lengths?

What are the characteristics of the tail?
Is it long? Is it short? Is it rounded? Is it forked?

What about the body?
Does the bird look rotund? Is it slim? Does the head look large in relation to the body size?

Movement
How a bird moves can also help you identify it. Ask yourself the following questions:

Does it walk? Does it hop? Is it mostly on the ground? Does it pump its tail? Does it crawl on tree trunks? Does it hang from branch tips?

A Brown Creeper (left) lives up to its name by creeping on tree trunks. Nuthatches (like this Red-breasted Nuthatch, right) creep on tree trunks, too, but they move and face any direction, whereas creepers stay upright. Unlike nuthatches, Brown Creepers also usually spiral upwards on the trunk and use their tails as props like a woodpecker.

Bird Anatomy and Field Marks

Field marks are the best way to start to identify your birds. Knowing where they are on the bird is important, too, so a little anatomy knowledge helps. And remember, the *lack* of a field mark can be just as important as the presence of one!

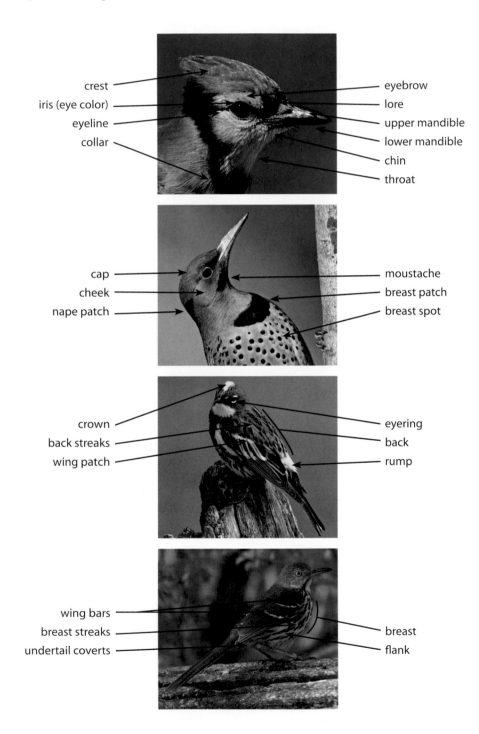

crest — eyebrow
iris (eye color) — lore
eyeline — upper mandible
collar — lower mandible
chin
throat

cap — moustache
cheek — breast patch
nape patch — breast spot

crown — eyering
back streaks — back
wing patch — rump

wing bars — breast
breast streaks — flank
undertail coverts

Maps

The maps should help you see what birds may be possible in your area. Remember that some species are habitat specific, so even if you are within a bird's range, your local ecosystem may not support it.

Legend

Red — Breeding Range (where the bird nests and raises young)

Blue — Wintering Range (where the bird is in the winter)

Yellow — Permanent Range (where the bird may be found all year)

Green — overlap if the map is covering more than one species

Dotted line — the general boundary between two species' ranges

Raptors and
Shrikes
(pp. *285–289*)

Titmice
(pp. *182–183,*
277)

Quail, Pheasants,
Grouse, Turkeys
and Chachalacas
(pp. *138–141,*
270–271)

Verdin and
Bushtit
(pp. 181)

Pigeons
and Doves
(pp. *144–149,*
270)

Nuthatches
(pp. 184–186)

Hummingbirds
(pp. *152–155,*
272–273)

Wrens and
Creeper
(pp. 187,
190–192, *277*)

Woodpeckers
(pp. *158–165,*
274–275)

Kinglets
(pp. 193)

Phoebes
(pp. *276*)

Solitaire and
Bluebirds
(pp. 194)

Jays
(pp. *168–171,*
277)

Thrushes
and Robin
(pp. 195–197)

Nutcracker
and Magpies
(pp. *172–173*)

Catbird and
Mockingbird
(pp. 200–201)

Crows and
Ravens
(pp. *174–175*)

Thrashers
(pp. *202–203,*
284)

Chickadees
(pp. 178–180)

Starling and
Waxwings
(pp. 204–205)

Rosy-Finches
(pp. 211)

"Red Finches"
(pp. 212–215)

Crossbills
(pp. 216)

Goldfinches
and Evening
Grosbeak
(pp. 217–219)

Redpolls
and Siskin
(pp. 220–221)

Warblers
(pp. 224–227,
282)

Towhees
and Juncos
(pp. 232–233,
237, *278–279*)

Sparrows
(pp. 210,
234–243, *279*,
280–281)

Lapland
Longspur and
Snow Bunting
(pp. *278*)

Tanagers
(pp. 246–247,
284)

Bird Quick-Find Guide

This short photographic guide will help you find which group an unfamiliar bird might belong to. Then you can check the page numbers listed here to see if your bird is described. Remember that some birds in your yard might not be in this book, so you may need to check a complete field guide of all North American birds. Pages set in *italics* are for the "More Feeder Birds" and "Predators" sections at the end of the bird identification pages.

Dickcissel,
Cardinal and
Pyrrhuloxia
(pp. 248–249,
279)

Grosbeaks
(pp. 252–253)

"Blue Buntings"
(pp. 254–255,
279)

Horned Lark and
Meadowlarks
(pp. 258, *276*)

Blackbirds
(pp. 259–263,
282–283)

Orioles
(pp. 266–269,
283)

California Quail
(male) (p. 138)
- Black topknot
- Beige forehead
- Black face
- Scaly lower breast
  and belly

California Quail
(female) (p. 138)
- Small black topknot
- Patterned nape
- Scaly lower breast
  and belly

Gambel's Quail
(male) (p. 138)
- Black topknot
- Black forehead
- Black face
- Plain lower breast

Gambel's Quail
(female) (p. 138)
- Small black topknot
- Fairly plain nape
- Plain lower breast

Gaudy Game Birds

You may find these chicken-like birds foraging on the ground under your feeders. They are large, chunky and often comical to watch.

Ruffed Grouse
(p. 139)
• Crest
• Pale eyeline
• Dark markings on nape

Wild Turkey
(p. 141)
• Mostly naked head
• Scaly, iridescent feathers

Ring-necked Pheasant
(male) (p. 140)
• Red face skin
• Pale beak
• Dark green head
• White neck ring

Ring-necked Pheasant
(female) (p. 140)
• Buffy with dark markings

California Quail and Gambel's Quail

Callipepla californica and *Callipepla gambelii*

THESE LITTLE GUYS always make me smile. They zip around, running from one bit of cover to the next, with their showy little topknots bobbing around on their foreheads. California Quail and Gambel's Quail are western birds that can be frequent feeder visitors. Gambel's Quail are usually found in more desert-like habitats. It can hybridize with California Quail where their ranges overlap.

Natural Foods

Mostly "weed" seeds; also seeds, flowers and/or leaves of woody plants such as poison oak, mesquite, juniper and poplar; new green growth, especially in late winter and early spring; some invertebrates

California

Gambel's

Feeder Fare

Millet, corn, sunflower seeds, water; feeds mostly on the ground

Female California Quail

Female Gambel's Quail

Male

CALIFORNIA QUAIL

Length: 10 inches (25.5 cm), shorter than Rock Pigeon

Topknot: black plumes on male; smaller on female

Cap: chestnut

Forehead: beige

Face: black with white outlines on male; no black on female

Body: gray and brown with scaled pattern on belly and central chestnut patch on male; browner overall and no chestnut patch on female

Male

GAMBEL'S QUAIL

Topknot: black plumes

Cap: chestnut

Forehead: black

Face: black with white outlines; no black on female

Body: gray with solid, creamy belly and no scaling, central black patch and chestnut patch on flanks; brown overall and no central patch on female

Neighborhood Watch: Sentinel Behavior

These plump little birds are on the menu for many animal species. One quail, usually a male, will sometimes perch in the open above a feeding or drinking flock and sound the alarm if it sees a predator.

Ruffed Grouse
Bonasa umbellus

Rufous phase

Gray phase

Length: 17 inches (43 cm), similar to American Crow
Gray phase is grayish-brown overall; Rufous phase is rufous brown overall
Crest
Neck: dark feathers on sides
Flank: thick, dark bars
Tail: barred with thick black subterminal band
Underparts: whitish and mottled

THE RUFFED GROUSE depends greatly on its amazing camouflage since it is a prey item for many predators: foxes, coyotes, goshawks, owls, lynx and bobcats. The gray phase is most common in the north, where its colors help it blend into the grays of spruce trunks and branches. In the south, the rufous phase allows the Ruffed Grouse to melt into the fallen deciduous leaves.

Natural Foods
Foliage; twigs; catkins; buds; seeds and/or fruit of plants such as aspen, oak, grape, greenbrier, clover, hazelnut, birch, willow, blueberry, hawthorn, dock, dogwood, cherry, blackberry and witch hazel

Feeder Fare
Cracked corn, seed mixes

Little Drummer Bird
The Ruffed Grouse has one of the most distinctive nonvocal natural sounds in North America. By beating its wings in front of its chest, it creates mini sonic booms as air rushes into the low-pressure areas it has created. It makes this drumroll effect by beating its wings about 50 times in 10 seconds. Male Ruffed Grouse use this drumming the same way that other birds use song: mate attraction and territorial rights.

Ring-necked Pheasant

Phasianus colchicus

Male

Female

AN ASIAN SPECIES successfully introduced to North America in 1882, the Ring-necked Pheasant can now be found in the central latitudes of the continent. Listen for the male pheasant's loud, hoarse, two-parted crowing at dawn and dusk in the spring.

Natural Foods

Insects, spiders, earthworms, snails, millipedes, toads, corn, ragweed, grape, skunk cabbage, oats, buckwheat, acorns, cherry, elderberry, blackberry, apple, wheat, sumac, beans, barley, dandelion, sunflower, knotweed, snowberry, strawberry

Feeder Fare

Cracked corn, seed mixes, sunflower seeds

Length: 21 inches (53 cm), longer than Red-tailed Hawk

Face: red skin on male

Head: male has shiny dark green, usually a white ring around neck

Body: rufous-brown with white and dark markings on male; brown overall on female

Upperparts: dark markings on female

Underparts: lighter on female

Tail: long, pointed, barred

My Best Side: The Lateral Display

This display shows off the male Ring-necked Pheasant's incredible plumage. He tilts his back toward the recipient of the display, either an intruding male he is trying to drive off or a female he is courting. If the audience is a female, the display could lead to mating. If the audience is a male, the display usually scares him off, but it may otherwise lead to a fight.

Wild Turkey
Meleagris gallopavo

Male

THESE HUGE BIRDS can really eat. One individual was found to have 221 large acorns in its crop (which is a swelling of the esophagus). But if they visit your feeding site, providing lots of seed is worth it for the chance to watch these birds' spectacular displays.

Length: 46 inches (117 cm)
Head: blue and red, with wattles on male; less blue and red and reduced wattles on female
Breast: center "beard" hangs from middle of breast on male (and some females)
Body: dark overall with green or purplish iridescence on male; browner overall on female, western females lighter than eastern
Wing: brown flight feathers barred with white
Tail: thin, dark bars with thick, dark subterminal band and white or rufous tip

Female

Natural Foods

Insects; spiders; crayfish; millipedes; centipedes; salamanders; acorns; seeds and/or fruits of plants such as beech, dogwood, hickory, hackberry, wheat, corn, grape, pine, elm, and oats

Feeder Fare

Corn, millet, seed mixes, sunflower seeds, safflower seeds

Displaying male

snood

wattle

caruncles

Nice Face!

Turkeys have some pretty cool head adornments. They can become swollen and/or more colorful during courtship displays. The snood is especially fun to watch. Dominant individuals can make their snood stand up on their beaks and may chase subordinate birds with their snood extended.

Rock Pigeon (p. 144)

• Variably gray, brown or white, or combinations of those colors

Delightful Doves

Usually found on the ground, these fast-flying birds have small heads for their size and short, tubular beaks. They are often found in flocks or pairs.

Band-tailed Pigeon (p. 271)
- Dark eye
- Yellow beak
- White nape band
- Gray breast with pink wash

Eurasian Collared-Dove (p. 145)
- Red eye
- Black beak
- Black nape band

Inca Dove (p. 146)
- Red eye
- Black beak
- Whitish face
- Scaly overall

Common Ground Dove (male) (p. 147)
- Red eye
- Red beak with black tip
- Bluish patterned nape
- Dark wing spots

White-tipped Dove (southern Texas only) (p. 271)
- Red eyering
- Pale eye
- Whitish face

White-winged Dove (p. 148)
- Blue eyering
- Red eye
- Black cheek mark
- White wing patch

Mourning Dove (adult) (p. 149)
- Dark eye
- Light blue eyering
- Dark cheek patch
- Black wing spots

Mourning Dove (juvenile) (p. 149)
- Dark eye
- Scaling on feathers

Rock Pigeon
Columba livia

ROCK PIGEONS HARDLY need an introduction — they are everywhere! But they weren't always. In fact, before the early 1600s, this species wasn't found in North America. Early settlers brought pigeons with them from Europe, and this very adaptable species soon became established across the continent. While not one of our most loved birds, pigeons are a great species to observe if you'd like to learn about bird behavior. Just sit in a local city park and start watching for courtship moves, preening techniques, flight displays and flock dynamics.

Natural Foods
Many different seeds and fruits, very few insects

Feeder Fare
Cracked corn, sunflower seeds, seed mixes, millet

Length: 12½ inches (32 cm)
Plumage colors and patterns are highly variable, but the following is most common:
Head: dark gray with greenish and/or purplish iridescence
Body: can be light gray, all dark, all brown, all white or pied combinations
Wing: two black wingbars
Rump: white
Tail: dark terminal band
Feet: reddish

Bowing, Tail Drag and Driving
One pigeon behavior to watch for from your park bench is "bowing." Males and females will fluff up their neck feathers and bow their heads while walking around in circles. A bowing male may add a "tail drag" by lifting up his head and then running forward while dragging his tail. He may also follow or "drive" his mate in front of him. This is part of the pigeon's courtship displays.

Many have a white rump.

There are many color variations.

Eurasian Collared-Dove

Streptopelia decaocto

ANOTHER MEMBER OF the pigeon family that was introduced from Europe, the Eurasian Collared-Dove was first released in North America in the Bahamas in the 1970s. Other introduction sites have led to the rapid spread of this species across much of North America. Eurasian Collared-Doves readily use bird feeders, so if you don't have some around already, you might soon!

Length: 13 inches (33 cm), similar to Rock Pigeon
Body: buffy-gray overall
Neck: dark band on back
Tail: white band at end, except central tail feathers

Natural Foods
Almost entirely seeds and fruits, very few insects

Feeder Fare
Various seed mixes

A Little to the Left … Ah, That's the Spot!

Birds mostly preen themselves with their beak. Unfortunately, this doesn't work for the bird's own head or neck since it can't reach these areas with its beak. In some species, one bird may preen another bird; this is called mutual preening or allopreening. Most allopreening concentrates on the partner's head and neck areas, as shown here by these two Eurasian Collared-Doves. While allopreening may occur between flock members or sometimes even different species, it is most often seen between mated individuals and likely strengthens their pair bond.

Inca Dove
Columbina inca

THE INCA DOVE is a small dove that has a long, tapering tail. It can be found in both arid and humid habitats, but its range is restricted to warm areas because it is sensitive to the cold. It has been known to decrease its body temperature up to 22°F (12°C) at night to conserve energy.

Natural Foods
Almost entirely plant materials, mostly seeds

Feeder Fare
Seed mixes, including sunflower seeds, millet, cracked corn and nyjer

Length: 8¼ inches (21 cm), shorter than Red-winged Blackbird
Body: buffy-gray overall, with dark edges to feathers
Eye: red
Beak: dark
Head: lighter
Wing: rufous primary feathers and underwing when viewed in flight
Tail: long for size, with white outer feathers

Dove Triangle
Inca Doves fight the cold by doing something called "pyramid roosting." The birds find a sunny branch and pile on top of each other, forming two or three rows. When the birds on the outside get too cold, they fly to the top and the pyramid members shift into new positions.

Common Ground-Dove

Columbina passerina

OUR SMALLEST DOVE is no longer than most sparrows. As its name suggests, this dove spends most of its time on the ground. It also nests on the ground, making it vulnerable to many different predators. To protect its eggs and nestlings, it is known to do a distraction display: it pretends to have a broken wing to get the predator to follow it, leading the predator away from its nest.

Length: 6 inches (15 cm), similar to Dark-eyed Junco
Crown and nape: bluish on male; no blue on female
Eye: red
Beak: red with black tip
Body: light brown overall on male; lighter overall on female
Wing: more rufous, dark spots, rufous primary feathers and underwing when viewed in flight
Underparts: more rufous
Tail: mostly dark, white tips on outside corners

Natural Foods

Seeds, berries, insects, snails

Feeder Fare

Hulled sunflower seeds, millet, cracked corn

Drinking Dove-Style

Pigeons and doves are able to suck up water instead of having to lower and raise their heads like other birds. Sucking up the water is very efficient, but it does make the bird vulnerable since it can't see approaching danger with its head down. Common Ground-Doves may protect themselves at watering sites by visiting in groups so that members who aren't drinking can watch for approaching predators.

White-winged Dove

Zenaida asiatica

Length: 11½ inches (29 cm), longer than Blue or Steller's Jay
Eye: red
Eyering: blue
Cheek: dark bar
Body: grayish-brown overall
Wing: white patch on edge (more visible during flight)
Tail: dark with white terminal band, except for central feathers

THIS DISTINCTIVE-LOOKING dove of the southernmost states can be found everywhere from sitting on top of a cactus in a remote desert to roaming around a populated city suburb. Its recent use of cityscapes has allowed this species to expand its range northward.

Natural Foods

Almost all plant material, such as seeds and/or fruits of acacia, cactus, oak, melons and prickly ash

Feeder Fare

Sunflower seeds, corn, safflower seeds, seed mixes

Cooing

Doves' cooing performs a similar function to singing in most of our feeder birds: to proclaim territory and attract mates. Male White-winged Doves have both a long cooing call and a short cooing call. They use the long call mostly for territorial purposes and the short call for communicating with their mate or a potential mate. In nesting colonies, where many birds may be calling at the same time, the resulting sound can be heard from over 3 miles (5 km) away!

Mourning Dove
Zenaida macroura

Adult

Juvenile

FOUND ACROSS THE lower 48 states and southern Canada, Mourning Doves are our most common native dove species. In fact, they are one of the most abundant birds in the United States. They often raise more than one brood per season; one Texas pair attempted to raise young six times in one year. This species is expanding northward, likely helped by bird feeders.

Length: 12 inches (30.5 cm), shorter than Rock Pigeon
Eye: dark
Eyering: light blue
Cheek: dark patch
Body: brown overall
Wing and lower back: brown with black spots
Tail: long and pointed, with white tips on outer feathers

Juvenile is similar to adult but has light edges on wing feathers

Natural Foods

Almost all plant material, including seeds and fruits of pigweed, ragweed, spurge, knotweed, poppy, thistle, mustard, pokeweed and crabgrass

Feeder Fare

Cracked corn, millet, seed mixes, sunflower seeds, safflower seeds

Flap-Glide Display

Male Mourning Doves sometimes perform a display in which they jump off their cooing perch and do some loud flapping before starting a long, spiraling, stiff-winged glide over their territory. These glides make them look surprisingly similar to a Sharp-shinned Hawk, so don't be fooled!

Black-chinned Hummingbird
(male) (p. 153)
- White spot behind eye
- Black chin
- Purple lower throat

Ruby-throated Hummingbird
(male) (p. 152)
- White spot behind eye
- Black mask
- Ruby-red throat

Broad-tailed Hummingbird
(male) (p. 272)
- White eyering
- White line on chin
- Pinkish-red throat

Rufous Hummingbird
(male) (p. 155)
- White spot behind eye
- Rufous head
- Orangish-red throat

Hovering Hummingbirds

Our smallest birds, hummers have very long, thin beaks and incredibly fast wings. They can also hover and fly in any direction, and their feathers are often iridescent. Females can be very hard to identify, so beginners should start with identifying the males.

Anna's Hummingbird
(male) (p. 154)
- White eyering
- Reddish-purple cap and throat
- Long feathers on side of throat

Costa's Hummingbird
(male) (p. 273)
- Thin white eyebrow
- Purple cap and throat
- Long feathers on side of throat

Calliope Hummingbird
(male) (p. 272)
- White spot behind eye
- Reddish-purple throat streaks

Buff-bellied Hummingbird
(p. 273)
- Buffy eyering
- Orange beak
- Green head

Ruby-throated Hummingbird

Archilochus colubris

THIS IS ONE of the most favorite birds in North America, or at least in eastern North America, as it is the only hummer regularly seen there. They are found as far north as the Great Lakes and up into Canada's prairie provinces and lower maritime provinces, giving northerners they're own flying jewel.

Natural Foods

Nectar, insects, spiders, tree sap

Feeder Fare

Sugar water

Male

Female

Oooooooh . . . Shiny!

Hummingbirds are one of the shiniest of all bird groups. The structure of their feathers causes light to refract, like a prism, creating brilliant colors. However, these iridescent colors only appear when the refracted light is at the right angle for the eye to see it. The colors produced can be visible at one angle but disappear at another, as shown by the red gorget on this male Ruby-throated Hummingbird. Depending on the species, male hummingbirds use their iridescent gorget to display to females and/or to intimidate other males.

Length: 3¾ inches (9.5 cm)
ADULT MALE
Mask: black
Throat: red
Tail: dark, pointed feathers
ADULT FEMALE
Crown and back: bright green
Mask: grayish
Throat: white
Tail: white tips on outer feathers, usually holds tail still while hovering

Black-chinned Hummingbird

Archilochus alexandri

Male

Female

WHILE MANY MALE hummers look like they have a black throat if the light doesn't hit it correctly, the Black-chinned Hummingbird actually does have a mostly black throat. However, the purple iridescent band along the bottom makes up for the lack of color further up, and it may even look more brilliant by having the deep black section next to it.

Natural Foods

Nectar, insects, spiders

Feeder Fare

Sugar water

Length: 3¾ inches (9.5 cm)

ADULT MALE

Mask and chin: black

Throat: purple

Tail: dark, pointed feathers

ADULT FEMALE

Crown: gray in front, bright green on back

Beak: longer than Ruby-throated Hummingbird

Face: pale

Throat: white

Tail: white tips on outer feathers, often pumps tail when hovering

Feathered Pollinators

This Black-chinned Hummingbird has pollen grains at the base of its beak. Hummingbirds co-evolved with flowers, forming a mutual partnership: hummers transport pollen from one flower to another in exchange for a meal of nectar. Many flowers are adapted specifically for hummingbird visitors; the stamens of these flowers can very effectively brush pollen onto birds' heads.

Anna's Hummingbird
Calypte anna

Male

Female

THE ANNA'S HUMMINGBIRD is one of the few bird species that has benefited from extensive plantings of non-native species. Originally only found in southern California and the Baja Peninsula, this hummingbird's range now extends all the way to Alaska.

Natural Foods
Nectar, insects, spiders

Feeder Fare
Sugar water

Length: 4 inches (10 cm), longer than Ruby-throated and Black-chinned Hummingbird
Crown: reddish-purple on male
Eyering: whitish
Eyebrow: white on female
Throat: reddish-purple on male; white with central dark pink patch on female
Back: green
Tail: rounded; black and gray feathers on male; white-tipped outer feathers on female

Allen's Hummingbird

Musical Feathers

While most bird species make display sounds with their voice, male hummingbirds can use special feathers to impress a potential mate or intimidate a male rival. Allen's Hummingbirds make these sounds by flying above the other hummingbird and vibrating their wing feathers, which in turn vibrate the air, creating chirping noises. Then they climb up to 100 feet (30 m) and do a spectacular high-speed dive. At the bottom of the dive, they spread their tail feathers out to make a loud whining sound as the air rushes past them. These are tiny birds with big talent!

Rufous Hummingbird and Allen's Hummingbird

Selasphorus rufus and *Selasphorus sasin*

Female

Male Allen's

Male Rufous

Male Rufous

THESE TWO HUMMINGBIRDS present one of the biggest identification challenges among North American birds. But even if you can't identify the one you are looking at, you can still enjoy it, as Thomas Nuttall did while watching a male Rufous Hummingbird: "In all the energy of life, it seemed like a breathing gem, or magic carbuncle of glowing fire, stretching out its gorgeous ruff, as if to emulate the sun itself in splendor" (Studer, 1881).

Natural Foods
Nectar, insects, tree sap

Feeder Fare
Sugar water

Allen's

Rufous

Length: 3¾ inches (9.5 cm), shorter than Ruby-throated and Black-chinned Hummingbird

MALE

Crown and back: usually rufous, sometimes with some green on Rufous; mostly green on Allen's

Throat: orangey-red

Breast: white upper

Belly: rufous

Tail: black-tipped, pointed feathers

FEMALE

Crown and back: green

Throat: whitish with grayish spots, central orangey-red patch

Flank: rufous

Tail: white tips and rufous bases on outer feathers

Anna's Hummingbird

Mine!
Male hummingbirds are *very* territorial. They often have a feeding territory as well as a courtship territory, which they defend from other hummingbirds. Some may even try to chase away birds as big as Northern Mockingbirds. Hummingbirds only really get together when males and females mate; no pair-bond is formed.

Red-headed Woodpecker
(p. 158)
- Red head
- Black back
- White wing patch
- White underparts

Acorn Woodpecker
(p. 159)
- Red cap (smaller on female)
- Creamy or white face and eye
- Black breast band and breast streaks
- White underparts

Red-bellied Woodpecker
(p. 160)
- Red cap and nape (less red on female)
- Black-and-white barred upperparts
- Beige face and underparts

Yellow-bellied Sapsucker
(p. 161)
- Red cap
- Black-and-white striped face
- Red throat on male (white throat on female)
- Black breast band
- Black-and-white barred back
- White wing patch
- Yellowish underparts

Wonderful Woodpeckers

Woodpeckers have long, strong and pointed beaks. They often perch vertically on tree trunks and brace themselves using their stiff tail feathers.

Downy Woodpecker
(p. 162)
- Short beak
- Black-and-white striped head and body
- Red patch on nape on male (no patch on female)
- White outer tail feathers, usually with black spots
- White underparts

Hairy Woodpecker
(p. 163)
- Long beak
- Black-and-white striped head and body
- Red patch on nape on male (no patch on female)
- White outer tail feathers, usually without black spots
- White underparts

Northern Flicker
(p. 164)
- Gray or brown face
- Red or black moustache on male (no moustache on female)
- Black breast patch
- Barred upperparts
- Yellow or reddish shafts on flight feathers
- White rump
- Spotted underparts

Pileated Woodpecker
(p. 165)
- Red crest on male (less red on female)
- Black-and-white striped head
- Black body

Red-headed Woodpecker

Melanerpes erythrocephalus

THIS COULD BE the easiest North American woodpecker to identify. Its fully red head and black-and-white body are quite distinctive. It is found over much of the eastern part of North America, particularly around oaks. It has been known to cover a stash of acorns with pieces of bark, either to hide them or to protect them from rain. They have also been observed placing nuts and pine cones on roads so that passing cars can crack them open! This ability to use tools shows how intelligent birds are, and it reveals how much we still have to learn about even the most common birds.

Natural Foods

Insects (including those in flight); spiders; acorns, beechnuts; corn; wild cherries, mulberries and other fruits; there are records of it eating other birds' nestlings and even mice!

Feeder Fare

Suet, peanuts, corn, sunflower seeds, suet/peanut butter spread

Length: 9¼ inch (23.5 cm), similar to Hairy Woodpecker
Head: bright red on adult; brown on juvenile
Upperparts: black on adult; brown on juvenile
Wing: large white patch
Rump: white
Underparts: white on adult; dirty white on juvenile

Heavy Metal Drummer

Woodpeckers often drum to claim territory as well as to court potential mates. Some individuals take advantage of aluminum siding, television antennae or metal stove pipes for drumming, likely because the resulting sound is louder and carries farther than the sounds they can make on deadwood. Woodpeckers are real headbangers!

Adult

Juvenile

Acorn Woodpecker
Melanerpes formicivorus

Male

Female

THIS IS A SOCIAL woodpecker that forms family groups of four to over a dozen individuals. The members help raise the young of one to three breeding females. Their survival largely rests on their ability to collect and store acorns, which make up over half of their diet.

Length: 9 inches (23 cm), similar to Hairy Woodpecker
Cap: red on male; smaller and red surrounded by black on female
Face: creamy or white
Eye: white
Breast: white with black band and black streaks
Upperparts: black
Wing: white patch
Rump: white
Underparts: whitish

Natural Foods
Insects, spiders, acorns, almonds, corn, walnuts

Feeder Fare
Suet, peanuts, suet/peanut butter spread, sugar water

Extreme Hoarders
Many bird species store food in anticipation of harder times, but Acorn Woodpeckers seem to take hoarding to a whole new level. They drill individual holes in trees to store acorns (and, to a lesser extent, other nuts). These holes can accumulate over generations and decades, and the birds often reuse them until the tree falls over. One such tree had at least 50,000 holes in it — that's a lot of acorns!

Red-bellied Woodpecker

Melanerpes carolinus

THIS WOODPECKER IS a favorite feeder visitor that never fails to garner "Ohs" and "Ahs" from observers. More and more people are now getting to experience this flashy species, as its range has been expanding northward since at least the early 1900s.

Natural Foods

Insects; spiders; acorns; seeds and/or fruits of plants such as grape, corn, mulberry, pine, Virginia creeper, cherry, hickory, bayberry and poison ivy

Feeder Fare

Suet, suet/peanut butter spread, sunflowers, peanuts, corn, fruits, sugar water

Length: 9¼ inches (23.5 cm), similar to Hairy Woodpecker

Crown: red on male; no red on female

Head: beige

Lore: orangey-red

Nape: red

Back: black-and-white bars

Rump: white with black flecks

Tail: usually black and white

Underparts: beige

Juveniles are similar to females but don't have red on their head

Male

Female

Juvenile

Beware of Woodpecker!

A recent study on dominance found that Red-bellied Woodpeckers are one of the most dominant common feeder birds, even beating out Blue Jays and European Starlings. All woodpeckers were found to be more dominant than their size would normally dictate. This is likely due to their strong beaks; would you want to fight a woodpecker the same size as you? This one is even fending off a predatory Loggerhead Shrike!

Red-naped Sapsucker and Yellow-bellied Sapsucker

Sphyrapicus nuchalis and *Sphyrapicus varius*

UNLIKE MOST WOODPECKERS, sapsuckers are uncommon visitors at feeding stations. They can, however, be attracted to trees for their sap. They have special beaks that are flattened sideways, which allows them to carve out wells through tree bark. They then visit these wells periodically to drink the sap, which can form 20 to 100 percent of their diet, depending on the time of year.

Male Red-naped   Female Red-naped

Natural Foods

Tree sap and some inner bark; insects, especially ants; fruits and/or seeds of plants such as dogwood, cherry, holly, Virginia creeper and juniper

Red-naped

Yellow-bellied

Feeder Fare

Suet, suet/peanut butter spread, fruits, sugar water

Male Yellow-bellied   Female Yellow-bellied   Juvenile Yellow-bellied

Well Done!

Sapsucker wells are important food sources for many wildlife species. Tanagers, phoebes, warblers, chickadees, nuthatches, hummingbirds and other woodpeckers have all been seen at sap wells. Non-birds like them, too, including squirrels, porcupines, butterflies, moths, wasps and bees. Sapsuckers will actively defend their wells, chasing these thieves away, but they can't be at all of their wells at once, so they end up providing a free meal to many.

Length: 8½ inches (21.5 cm), shorter than Hairy Woodpecker
Face: black-and-white stripes; some red on cheeks on male Red-naped
Nape: red on Red-naped; usually white on Yellow-bellied
Chin: red on male; white on female
Throat: red; all white on female Yellow-bellied
Back: black-and-white bars; more white on Yellow-bellied
Breast: black
Underparts: white or yellowish with black barring
Wing: black with white patch
Tail: barred
Juveniles are similar to adults but have a browner head and underparts and little to no red

Downy Woodpecker
Dryobates pubescens

OUR SMALLEST WOODPECKER is also the one most commonly seen at bird feeders. Away from feeders, Downy Woodpeckers are often part of mixed-species feeding flocks that may include chickadees, titmice, nuthatches and Brown Creepers.

Natural Foods
Insects; spiders; seeds; sap; fruits of plants such as poison ivy, mulberry and dogwood

Feeder Fare
Suet, suet/peanut butter spread, sunflower seeds, safflower seeds, seed mixes, peanuts, corn, fruits, sugar water

Length: 6¾ inches (17 cm)
Face: black-and-white stripes
Beak: short
Nape: red patch on male
Back: white bordered with black
Wing: black with white spotting; western birds may have less white spotting
Underparts: white; Pacific northwestern birds may be beige instead of white
Tail: black with white outer feathers with black spots
Juveniles are similar to females but have a streaky red crown

Male

Female

Juvenile

They Have the Gall To . . .
If you have ever been in a field of goldenrod in the winter, you might have noticed round balls on some of the stems. These are called galls, and inside them live a fly larva that will pupate and emerge in the spring. Downy Woodpeckers have figured out that these little spheres contain a nice, protein-rich snack, so they balance on the thin stem and peck out the larva. Chickadees also do this, but they have to tear at the sphere a bit more to get at the prize inside. You can tell which bird has been feeding on the gall larva because of their different feeding techniques. The upper photo shows where a Downy Woodpecker was the predator, and the lower shot shows a chickadee's handiwork.

Hairy Woodpecker

Dryobates villosus

Male

Female

Juvenile

HAIRY WOODPECKERS LOOK a bit like Downy Woodpeckers on steroids, and, like their smaller counterparts, they are also found across most of North America. Unlike most woodpeckers, however, this species often prefers to excavate its nesting cavity in a living — rather than dead — tree.

Length: 9¼ inches (23.5 cm)
Face: black-and-white stripes
Beak: long
Nape: red patch on male
Back: white bordered with black
Wing: black with white spotting; western birds may have less white spotting
Underparts: white; Pacific northwestern birds may be beige instead of white
Tail: black with white outer feathers; rarely with black spots
Juveniles are similar to females but have a streaky red crown

Natural Foods

Insects; spiders; millipedes; seeds and/or fruits of plants such as poison ivy

Feeder Fare

Suet, suet/peanut butter spread, sunflower seeds, safflower seeds, seed mixes, peanuts, corn

Western male

V-Wing Display

This young Hairy Woodpecker is doing a "V-wing" display. It had just started feeding at one of my feeders and was obviously nervous about being out in the open. When a Mourning Dove flew by to land on my hopper feeder, the Hairy Woodpecker perceived it as a threat and tried to intimidate it with a V-wing display. They also use this display to show aggression to other Hairy Woodpeckers, and parents use it to defend their nest from potential predators.

Northern Flicker

Colaptes auratus

Male (*left*), female (*center*) and in flight (*right*) "Red-shafted"

Male (*left*), female (*center*) and in flight (*right*) "Yellow-shafted"

Length: 12½ inches (32 cm), longer than Hairy Woodpecker
Brownish overall
Moustache: red or black on male
Beak: long
Nape: red crescent (northern and eastern areas only)
Breast: black spots and black patch
Belly: black spots
Back: black bars
Rump: white
Wing: red or yellow feathers visible in flight

THIS FLASHY WOODPECKER comes in two flavors for your enjoyment. In the west, the wing and tail flight feathers are red (so it is known as "Red-shafted"), and the male sports a red moustache. In the east, the Northern Flicker has a red nape crescent and yellow wing and tail flight feathers (yup, you guessed it, it is known as the "Yellow-shafted"), and the male has a black moustache. Where the ranges of these two forms meet, you may see combined characteristics and/or orangish flight feathers. Northern Flickers are often seen on the ground eating one of their main foods: ants.

Natural Foods

Insects (especially ants), some seeds and fruits

Feeder Fare

Suet, suet/peanut butter spread, sunflower seeds, millet, peanuts, corn

On the Tip of Its Tongue

Woodpeckers have lots of great adaptations, but their tongue might be the coolest one of all. They are *very* long: a flicker can extend its tongue almost 2 inches (5 cm) past the tip of its beak. Depending on the species, a woodpecker's tongue could be sticky (which flickers use to catch ants), barbed (which many woodpeckers use to skewer wood-boring beetle larvae) or brushed and tubular (which sapsuckers use to lap up sap). To store all of that tongue, it is wrapped internally from the woodpecker's beak, under its lower mandible, behind its skull and past its forehead, where it attaches around its eye orbit or nostril!

Pileated Woodpecker

Dryocopus pileatus

THIS IS ONE of the most impressive bird species that might visit your feeder. Looking more like a pterodactyl in flight than a modern bird, they will swoop in for suet, especially if it is offered in a feeder big enough to accommodate their large size. If you are really lucky, you might even get the whole family visiting once the chicks are old enough . . . One can dream!

Male

Female

Length: 16½ inches (42 cm), shorter than American Crow
Cap and crest: red; less red on females
Head: black-and-white stripes
Forehead: red on male; black on female
Moustache: red on male; black on female
Body: black with white stripe on sides of neck
Wing: white patch; white lining visible in flight

Natural Foods

Insects, especially carpenter ants; fruits and/or seeds of plants such as grape, black gum, Virginia creeper, sassafras, holly, elderberry and cherry

Feeder Fare

Suet, suet/peanut butter spread, sometimes sunflower seeds and seed mixes

Deluxe Room Vacancy

Old woodpecker holes are often used as nesting sites by other birds. However, Pileated Woodpecker cavities are big enough to accommodate very large residents. Here, a Northern Saw-whet Owl looks out of an old Pileated Woodpecker cavity. Other owl species — such as Boreal, Flammulated, Eastern Screech- and Western Screech-Owls — as well as American Kestrels and even ducks — such as Wood Ducks, Buffleheads and Common Goldeneyes — have voted the Pileated Woodpecker their favorite landlord!

Blue Jay
(p. 170)
• Blue crest
• Black collar
• Bright blue upperparts
• Light gray underparts

Steller's Jay
(p. 170)
• Black crest
• Black head
• Blue upperparts
• Blue underparts

Pinyon Jay
(p. 169)
• No crest
• Plain face
• Blue upperparts
• Blue underparts

**Scrub-Jay
(three species)**
(p. 171)
• No crest
• Gray back patch
• Blue upperparts
• White or gray
  underparts

Crafty Crows and Joyful Jays

Corvids (which include ravens, crows, jays, magpies and nutcrackers) are often found in flocks. They have many different calls. They are very intelligent and use their brainpower to not only procure food but also remember where they stored it.

Canada Jay
(p. 168)
- Gray hind crown
- Whitish head
- Dark gray upperparts
- Whitish underparts

Black-billed Magpie
(p. 173)
- Black head
- White belly and shoulder
- Bluish-green wing
- Long bluish-green tail

Crow (three species)
(p. 174)
- All black
- Large beak

Common Raven
(p. 175)
- All black
- Very large beak
- Pointed throat feathers

Canada Jay
Perisoreus canadensis

YOU WON'T FIND a friendlier bird than the Canada Jay (formerly called Gray Jay). If you've ever gone for a fall or winter hike in a mountainous area or in the boreal forest, this curious mooch may well have crashed your day out. They'll happily take trail mix, berries or even part of your sandwich right from your outstretched hand and hide it away for future consumption. Their friendliness and intelligence may soon earn this species the title of "National Bird of Canada."

Natural Foods
Insects, spiders, berries, fungus, carrion, eggs, nestlings, small amphibians

Feeder Fare
Suet, suet/peanut butter spread, peanuts, raisins, sunflower seeds, seed mixes

Size: 11½ inches (29 cm), similar to Blue and Steller's Jay
Beak: short compared to other jays
Hind cap and upper nape: variable amounts of black or dark gray
Lower nape: white
Upperparts: dark gray
Underparts: light gray or whitish
Juveniles are dark gray overall and have a whitish moustache

Adult

Juvenile

A common feeding place!

Freezing Cold? Snow Problem!
Canada Jays start nesting *way* before other songbirds; females might be sitting on eggs as early as mid-February, when there is still very deep snow in their range. The females do all of the incubation and keep snow off the eggs and nestlings. Canada Jays store a lot of food during the summer and fall. It is thought that they may breed very early in order to give their young lots of time to store food so they can survive their first winter.

Pinyon Jay
Gymnorhinus cyanocephalus

THIS ALL-BLUE jay is very social and flocks can contain over 500 members! Yearling male birds may help their parents feed their younger siblings while the chicks are in the nest.

Length: 10½ inches (27 cm), shorter than Blue and Steller's Jay
Dusky blue overall
Head: brighter blue
Tail: brighter blue, short

Natural Foods
Mostly pine seeds; sometimes seeds of plants such as cedar, wheat and corn; insects

Feeder Fare
Sunflower seeds, peanuts, seed mixes, possibly corn, possibly suet and suet/peanut butter spread

Throat Pouch
Pinyon Jays and Pinyon Pines have co-evolved and have a mutually beneficial relationship: the trees provide seeds that are a food source for the jays, and the jays provide a transportation and planting service for the trees (the birds store seeds in the ground for later consumption, but they don't actually consume all of them, so some grow into trees). To help this process along, the Pinyon Jay has an expandable esophagus that forms a throat pouch big enough to hold up to 40 pine seeds!

Steller's Jay and Blue Jay

Cyanocitta stelleri and *Cyanocitta cristata*

Steller's Jay

Steller's Jay

Blue Jay

THE STELLER'S JAY — found mostly in the west — is well known for its loud calls, which it directs at anything it thinks is intruding on its territory or that it finds irritating. Thomas Nuttall noted, "So intent are they on vociferating, that it is not uncommon to hear them busily scolding, even while engaged with a large acorn in the mouth" (Studer, 1881). Blue Jays are the Steller's counterpart in the forests of central and eastern North America. They are also sentinels of great renown.

Natural Foods

Insects; nestlings; eggs; frogs; mice; acorns; seeds and/or fruits of plants such as beech, blackberry, elderberry, cherry, oats, wheat, raspberry, pine and grape

Blue

Steller's

Feeder Fare

Sunflower seeds, peanuts, seed mixes, corn, suet, suet/peanut butter spread, sugar water

STELLER'S JAY
Length: 11½ inches (29 cm)
Head: black with prominent crest; some populations have white markings on face
Shoulders and breast: gray
Belly, wings and tail: blue
BLUE JAY
Length: 11 inches (28 cm)
Cap: blue, prominent crest
Face: white
Lore and eyeline: black
Collar: black
Upperparts: bright blue
Underparts: light gray
Wing: black-and-white markings
Tail: blue with black bars and white tips

Memory Masters

Jays, nutcrackers, crows, ravens and chickadees are incredibly talented at remembering where they have stored food. Their spatial memory allows them to cache thousands of food items in the fall and find them again during the winter. They can also remember where they have seen other birds stash food so they can steal it later.

California Scrub-Jay, Woodhouse's Scrub-Jay and Florida Scrub-Jay

Aphelocoma californica, Aphelocoma woodhouseii and *Aphelocoma coerulescens*

California Scrub-Jay

Woodhouse's Scrub-Jay

Florida Scrub-Jay

THESE JAYS USED to be classified as the same species, but they have recently been divided into three separate species. This is called "splitting," and it is based on current research about their genetics, their lives and how much they may interbreed.

Size: 11½ (29 cm), similar to Blue and Steller's Jay
Cheek: dark gray on California and Woodhouse's; blue on Florida
Eyebrow: thin, white
Forehead: blue on California and Woodhouse's; white on Florida
Throat: white
Breast: blue band; faint on Woodhouse's
Back: brownish-gray patch
Upperparts: bright blue on California and Florida; duller on Woodhouse's
Underparts: whitish on California; grayer on Woodhouse's; beige on Florida

California

Florida

Woodhouse's

Natural Foods
Insects; spiders; nestlings; eggs; acorns; seeds and/or fruits of plants such as cherry, pine, corn, raspberry, oats and gooseberry

Feeder Fare
Sunflower seeds, peanuts, seed mixes, corn, suet, suet/peanut butter spread

Color Banding
Becoming familiar with individual birds (see pages 104–106) can open up a whole new level of behavior and natural history exploration. Scientists make birds individually identifiable by putting a distinct, colored band combination on both legs. This allows researchers to study who is paired with whom, whose territory is whose, return rates after migration and even individual personality traits. Some bird populations have been studied for decades, giving us unprecedented views into their lives.

Clark's Nutcracker

Nucifraga columbiana

NAMED AFTER WILLIAM Clark, of the famous Lewis and Clark duo, this is one of only two nutcracker species found in the world. Clark's Nutcrackers are such pine seed specialists that they have formed a symbiotic relationship with some western pine species. These pines produce wingless seeds because they depend on the nutcrackers to disperse them.

Natural Foods
Mostly pine seeds but also insects, small mammals and carrion

Feeder Fare
Peanuts, suet/peanut butter spread, sunflower seeds, mealworms

Length: 12 inches (30.5 cm), longer than Blue and Steller's Jay
Face: white
Body: light gray
Wing: black with white patch
Tail: black with white outer feathers
Undertail coverts: white

Identification During Flight
Sometimes birds zip by so quickly that it can be difficult to identify them. However, you can identify birds in flight if you know what to look for. For example, a flying Clark's Nutcracker has an all-gray head and body, dark wings and a trailing white edge on its secondary feathers. It also has white outer tail feathers and a long, pointed beak. Flight ID takes practice, but learning how to do it can help you identify your feeder visitors.

Black-billed Magpie and Yellow-billed Magpie

Pica hudsonia and *Pica nuttalli*

Black-billed

Black-billed

Yellow-billed

A BEAUTIFUL MEMBER of the corvid family, Black-billed Magpies range over much of the west. They constantly search for feeding opportunities and are particularly fond of carrion. Like other corvids, magpies store food and will steal food stored by other birds when they can. To prevent this, the magpie that arrives first at a carrion site will often store food close by. When another magpie shows up, the first magpie will then store food farther away because it will be harder for subsequent magpies to find it. Later, the first magpie digs up the food it initially stored, near the carcass, and moves it closer to its nest. Smart! Yellow-billed Magpies are closely related to the Black-billed but have a restricted range in central California.

Natural Foods

Carrion; insects; ticks; small mammals; nestlings; eggs; fruit and/or seeds of plants such as wheat, cherry, serviceberry, hackberry and gooseberry

Feeder Fare

Peanuts, suet, suet/peanut butter spread, sunflower seeds, corn

Length:
Black-billed: 19 inches (48 cm)
Yellow-billed: 16½ inches (42 cm)
Head and body: black
Beak and eyering: black on Black-billed; yellow on Yellow-billed
Belly and shoulder: white
Wing: bluish-green; white in primary feathers when viewed in flight
Tail: bluish-green, very long

Black-billed
Yellow-billed

Mammal Munchies

Black-billed Magpies are known to eat ticks off of large ungulates, such as deer, elk (shown here) and moose. This is beneficial to both: the bird gets a meal, and the elk gets rid of a pesky parasite. However, magpies often remove a tick, fly off and bury it for later consumption. If the bird doesn't reclaim its prize, the tick may lay its eggs and produce many more ticks . . . Good for the magpie, but not for the elk, deer or moose!

American Crow, Fish Crow and **Northwestern Crow**

Corvus brachyrhynchos, Corvus ossifragus and *Corvus caurinus*

THESE THREE BIRDS look so similar that you might need to use range maps or calls to help you with your identification. Regardless of the exact species, crows are amazingly diverse in their food choices: they are true food generalists. They are also very intelligent and can figure out how to get to that food, so be sure to keep your garbage in crow-proof containers!

Length:
American: 17½ inches (44.5 cm)
Fish and Northwestern: 15–16 inches (38–40.5 cm)
All black
Beak: large
Wing: longer on Fish
Tail: rounded on American; longer on Fish; shorter on Northwestern
Call: American's common call is "caw"; Fish is higher and more nasally "caw-ah"; Northwestern is lower and rougher "caw"

Natural Foods

Almost everything! Insects, marine life, small mammals, carrion, birds, birds' and turtles' eggs, reptiles, amphibians, fish, fruits, seeds, human foods

Feeder Fare

Corn; peanuts; possibly seed mixes, suet, suet/peanut butter spread, fruits

Northwestern

American

■ both American and Fish

Size Comparison

Judging size can be quite difficult in certain situations, making identification challenging. But if there is another familiar bird nearby, its size can be a helpful reference. For example, is this Bald Eagle being attacked by a crow or a raven? A Bald Eagle has a wingspan of 80 inches (203 cm), a raven has a wingspan of 53 inches (135 cm) and a crow has a wingspan of 39 inches (99 cm). As we can see by comparing the wingspans of the two birds, this is a crow.

Common Raven

Corvus corax

THE COMMON RAVEN is the largest songbird in the world and one of the most intelligent birds. They will sometimes work as a team to get food, such as one bird distracting another animal while a second raven steals its food. They have also been known to follow wolves or cougars so they can get the leftovers after the predators have made a kill. Common Ravens also store nonedible items when other ravens are watching in the hopes of fooling the would-be thieves. If a raven is coming to your feeder, watch it carefully and see if you can observe any of its decision-making processes in action.

Length: 24 inches (61 cm), longer than Red-tailed Hawk
All black
Beak: very large and heavy looking
Throat: feathers are very pointed (not always visible)
Tail: wedge shaped

Natural Foods

Mainly carrion but also insects, marine life, small mammals, birds, birds' eggs, fruits, seeds, human foods

Feeder Fare

Possibly corn, suet, mixed seeds, suet/peanut butter spread

Show Off!

Ravens seem to revel in showing off to each other, doing dives and barrel rolls and swoops. But, as one of the most intelligent birds, they also seem to be able to understand things. I was once leading a hike when a single raven flew toward my group. As it approached, it suddenly rolled onto its back and actually flew upside down. After a few flaps, it righted itself and flew over our heads as if it not only knew we couldn't fly but knew that we were jealous.

Carolina Chickadee
(p. 178)
- Black cap
- Black throat with distinct, straight boundary along lower edge
- Gray at sides of nape
- Gray upperparts
- Very little white edging on wing feathers

Black-capped Chickadee (p. 178)
- Black cap
- Black throat with indistinct, jagged boundary along lower edge
- White at sides of nape
- Gray upperparts
- Prominent white edging on wing feathers

Chestnut-backed Chickadee (p. 180)
- Dark brown cap
- Dark brown throat
- White at sides of nape
- Chestnut back

Boreal Chickadee
(p. 180)
- Brown cap
- Dark brown throat
- Gray at sides of nape
- Brown upperparts
- Orangish side
- Prominent white edging on wing feathers

Mountain Chickadee
(p. 179)
- Black cap
- White eyebrow
- Black eyeline
- Black throat
- White at sides of nape
- Gray upperparts

Bushtit (p. 181)
- Grayish overall
- Some have brownish cap
- Females have light eye

Verdin (p. 181)
- Gray overall
- Yellow head
- Chestnut wing patch

Brown Creeper
(p. 187)
- Brown head
- Light eyebrow
- Thin, curved beak
- Mottled brown upperparts with white flecks
- White underparts
- Pointed tail feathers

Chickadees, Titmice and **Nuthatches**

These small birds include some of backyard birders' favorite species. Many travel in mixed-species flocks, and some are very good at storing an incredible number of food items.

Tufted Titmouse (p. 183)
- Gray overall
- Long crest
- Black forehead
- Orangey flanks

Black-crested Titmouse (p. 183)
- Gray overall
- Long black crest
- Orangey flank

Oak Titmouse (p. 182)
- Brownish-gray overall
- Short crest
- Plain face

Juniper Titmouse (p. 182)
- Grayish overall
- Short crest
- Plain face

White-breasted Nuthatch (p. 185)
- Black or gray cap
- White face
- Bluish upperparts
- White underparts

Red-breasted Nuthatch (p. 184)
- Black or gray cap
- White eyebrow
- Black eyeline
- Bluish upperparts
- Orangish underparts

Pygmy Nuthatch (p. 186)
- Brownish-gray cap
- Dusky eyeline
- Bluish-gray upperparts
- Buffy underparts

Brown-headed Nuthatch (p. 186)
- Brownish cap
- Dusky eyeline
- Bluish-gray upperparts
- Light buffy underparts

Carolina Chickadee
and **Black-capped Chickadee**
Poecile carolinensis and *Poecile atricapillus*

THE BLACK-CAPPED Chickadee — or its look-alike, the Carolina Chickadee — is one of the top-two feeder birds across North America, except in the southwest (explore feederwatch. org to find your region's top 25). These birds are bold and often the first species to be enticed to land on your hand. They are also one of the birds most likely to use your nest box.

Natural Foods
Insects; spiders; insect and spider eggs; seeds and/or fruits of plants such as pine, hemlock, birch, poison ivy and yew

Black-capped

Carolina

Feeder Fare
Sunflower seeds, safflower seeds, hulled peanuts, suet, suet/peanut butter spread

Length:
Black-capped: 5¼ inches (13.5 cm)
Carolina: 4¾ inches (12 cm)
Cap: black
Throat: black; Carolina usually has a more distinct, straight boundary along lower edge
Cheek: white; grayish near nape on Carolina; white near nape on Black-capped
Flank: may be buff on Carolina; brighter buffy coloring on Black-capped
Upperparts: gray
Wing: thin whitish edges on flight feathers on Carolina; brighter white edges on Black-capped
Underparts: whitish
Call: Carolina's is higher pitched and less harsh than Black-capped
Song: Carolina has four- or five-note song; Black-capped has two- or three-note song

Drip, Drip, Drip
Getting water can sometimes be a challenge, but this chickadee has found a handy spot to grab a drop or two! Some birds have figured out to wait at dripping water fountains or outdoor taps to get the moisture they need. In the early spring in northern regions, you may see birds getting drips of sweet sap water from a "sapcicle" hanging from a tree branch.

Mountain Chickadee

Poecile gambeli

THE "ANGRY" EYEBROWS of the Mountain Chickadee distinguish it from the Black-capped Chickadee, its close relative. A widespread chickadee of western mountainous regions, this species may hybridize with Black-capped Chickadees in some parts of its range.

Size: 5¼ inches (13.5 cm), similar to Black-capped Chickadee
Cap: black
Eyebrow: white; variable in thickness depending on location
Eyeline: black
Cheek: white
Throat: black
Upperparts: gray
Underparts: whitish

Natural Foods

Insects, spiders, seeds and/or fruits of plants such as pine and poison oak

Feeder Fare

Sunflower seeds, hulled peanuts, suet, suet/peanut butter spread

Hooray — I Have a Cavity!

Cavity nests are one of those good and bad things. The bad part: finding one can be very challenging, as other cavity-nesting species also want one. Birds often fight for possession of these rare resources. The good part: cavity nests offer very good protection for eggs and nestlings. Few predators can reach inside them, and they offer better shelter from the weather than conventional nests. Because of this protection, cavity nesters, on average, take longer to fledge their young — there's no rush to leave!

Chestnut-backed Chickadee and **Boreal Chickadee**

Poecile rufescens and *Poecile hudsonicus*

THESE TWO SPECIES add some nice browns and beiges to the often-monochrome appearance of the other chickadees. Unlike the other three chickadees in this book, these two don't have a distinctive whistled song (like the commonly heard two-toned "cheeeese burger" song of the Black-capped Chickadee). They do, however, have many complex calls, like other chickadees.

Natural Foods

Insects, spiders, insect and spider eggs, seeds, buds, fruits

Boreal

Chestnut-backed

Feeder Fare

Sunflower seeds, suet, suet/peanut butter spread, hulled peanuts

■ both

CHESTNUT-BACKED
Length: 4¾ inches (12 cm), smaller than Black-capped Chickadee
Cap: dark
Cheek: white
Throat: dark
Back: chestnut
Flanks: chestnut, lighter in some populations
Underparts: whitish or gray

Getting a Foothold

Birds process the foods they eat in many ways. Some just use their beaks, and some wedge their prize into a crack and then hammer it open. Chickadees depend on their feet for much of their feeding. Watch your feeder chickadees, and you will see that they often fly in, grab a seed with their beak, fly to a perch, transfer the seed to their feet and then peck it open and break off pieces to swallow.

BOREAL
Length: 5½ inches (14 cm), similar to Black-capped Chickadee
Cap: brown
Cheek: white blending to gray near nape
Throat: dark
Back: grayish-brown
Flanks: brownish
Underparts: whitish

Verdin and Bushtit

Auriparus flaviceps and *Psaltriparus minimus*

Adult Verdin

Female Bushtit

Male Bushtit

Male Bushtit

VERDINS ARE SMALL, desert-loving birds that usually roam in ones or twos as they forage for insects. In contrast, Bushtits are found in forests and shrubby areas and are very social, moving around in flocks of 10 to 40 members.

Length: 4½ inches (11.5 cm), smaller than Black-capped Chickadee
VERDIN
Head: yellow on male; duller on female
Shoulder: rufous patch on male; duller patch on female
Upperparts: gray
Underparts: whitish
Juveniles are gray overall and have a plain face.
BUSHTIT
Cap: brownish in Pacific population
Eye: dark on male; light on female
Cheek: may have partial or full black patch
Head and Upperparts: gray
Underparts: brownish or grayish

Natural Foods

Verdin: insects; spiders; insect and spider eggs; nectar; seeds and/or fruits of plants such as palm, hackberry, mesquite, wolfberry and paloverde
Bushtit: insects, spiders, some seeds, some fruits

Feeder Fare

Verdin: fruits, mealworms, suet/ peanut butter spread, sugar water
Bushtit: suet, suet/peanut butter spread, possibly sunflower seeds

Verdin

Bushtit

Nectar Thief

While many plants have developed flowers with special shapes and colors to attract insects, plants with red flowers are often trying to attract birds, such as hummingbirds, to their nectar. In exchange, the birds often inadvertently carry pollen from one flower to another, helping the plants reproduce. But some birds are nectar thieves. This Verdin has made a small hole at the base of the flower and is getting nectar through it, bypassing the pollen-covered anthers. But in this case, all is not lost for the plant. Its anthers stick out just enough that the pollen may end up being transferred to the Verdin's breast and belly feathers, which will transport it from plant to plant.

Oak Titmouse and Juniper Titmouse

Baeolophus inornatus and *Baeolophus ridgwayi*

Oak Titmouse

Juniper Titmouse

DO THESE BIRDS look the same to you? They look the same to me! There are some slight differences, but your best bet is to look at their range maps and to listen to their call notes. They used to be considered the same species, called the Plain Titmouse, but recent studies show that differences in genetics, habitats and vocalizations separate them into two species.

Natural Foods
Insects; spiders; acorns; fruits and/or seeds of plants such as pine, poison oak, thistle and weeds; buds; catkins; galls

Feeder Fare
Sunflower seeds, suet/peanut butter spread, suet, safflower seeds

Length: 5¾ inches (14.5 cm), longer than Black-capped Chickadee
Crest: small
Face: plain
Body: brownish-gray overall
Call: Oak's is a fast, very high, thin "see-see-see-see burrr"; Juniper's is fast, harsh chatter

Oak

Juniper

All Right, Leftovers Again!
Acorns pack a lot of energy but can be tough nuts to crack. This Oak Titmouse has saved itself a lot of work by searching for a spot where an Acorn Woodpecker has just finished feeding. The titmouse will greatly benefit from any leftovers since they don't require it to use up extra energy.

Tufted Titmouse and Black-crested Titmouse

Baeolophus bicolor and *Baeolophus atricristatus*

THESE PERKY LITTLE titmice are often members of mixed winter foraging flocks. Other members may include Downy Woodpeckers, White-breasted Nuthatches, Pine Warblers, Ruby-crowned Kinglets and Black-capped or Carolina Chickadees. The titmice dominate members such as the chickadees, which give the titmice greater access to better food sources, which helps improve their body condition.

Tufted Titmouse

Black-crested Titmouse

Length: 6½ inches (16.5 cm), longer than Black-capped Chickadee
Crest: gray on Tufted; black on Black-crested
Forehead: black on Tufted; pale on Black-crested
Face: white
Upperparts: gray
Flanks: light orange
Underparts: white

Black-crested

Tufted

Natural Foods
Insects; spiders; acorns; beechnuts; fruits and/or seeds of plants such as corn, apple, blackberry and blueberry

Feeder Fare
Sunflower seeds, peanuts, suet/peanut butter spread, safflower seeds, suet

Photo Fun
Feeders not only allow you to get a good look at birds, but they can also be great places for you to take photos of them. And why not have a little fun while you are at it? Put seeds in interesting places and have your camera ready for a photo that will be shared by all your friends on social media!

Red-breasted Nuthatch

Sitta canadensis

Male

Female

FOUND IN MOST of North America, this nuthatch's bright colors and humorous little "yank" calls attract the attention of numerous backyard birders. Like chickadees, they are most likely to land on a feeder, grab a seed and fly off to eat it elsewhere. Only suet seems to entice them to stick around, so they can hammer off the good bits.

Natural Foods

Insects; spiders; seeds of plants such as pine, spruce, cypress and sedge; maple buds; occasionally fruits

Feeder Fare

Suet, sunflower seeds, suet/peanut butter spread, hulled peanuts, jelly

Length: 4½ inches (11.5 cm), shorter than Black-capped Chickadee
Cap: black on male; gray on female
Eyebrow: white
Eyeline and cheek: black
Upper throat and lower cheek: white
Upperparts: bluish
Tail: short
Underparts: orange on male; paler orange on female
Movement: any direction on tree trunks

Sticky Situation

Red-breasted Nuthatches are known to add conifer resin to the edges of the entrance to their cavity nest. They apply the resin with their beaks or, sometimes, use a piece of bark to spread the resin (tool use!). Experiments have shown that nest-site competitors, such as House Wrens, and predators, such as Red Squirrels and Deer Mice, avoid cavities with resin. It looks like Red-breasted Nuthatches have useful decorating techniques!

White-breasted Nuthatch

Sitta carolinensis

Male

Female

OUR LARGEST NUTHATCH, the White-breasted is more often found in deciduous forests than the Red-breasted Nuthatch, which prefers more coniferous-rich forests. Both can be found in mixed forests. White-breasted Nuthatches store lots of seeds in crevices in bark. One year, my dad and I had to take down a large wind-damaged Yellow Birch in our yard, and when it hit the ground the bark exploded with sunflower seeds! I'm sure the local White-breasted Nuthatch was not happy with us.

Length: 5¾ inches (14.5 cm), longer than Black-capped Chickadee
Cap: black on male; gray on female
Face: white
Flanks: grayish
Upperparts: bluish
Undertail coverts: chestnut and white
Underparts: white
Movement: any direction on tree trunks

Natural Foods

Insects; spiders; fruits and/or seeds of plants such as pine, corn, oats, grape and hawthorn

Feeder Fare

Suet, sunflower seeds, suet/peanut butter spread, hulled peanuts

Back Off!

As you might have guessed, this White-breasted Nuthatch is *not* happy! This wing-spread display is an aggressive move that you may see near your feeder; it shows that the nuthatch is competing with another feeder visitor for a choice food or prize feeding spot.

Pygmy Nuthatch and Brown-headed Nuthatch

Sitta pygmaea and *Sitta pusilla*

Pygmy Nuthatch

Brown-headed Nuthatch

NUTHATCHES ARE SOMETIMES called "bottoms-up" birds because of their characteristic foraging techniques. They are often seen climbing down tree trunks headfirst. This allows them to find food in crevices that are missed by other trunk feeders, such as woodpeckers and creepers.

Natural Foods
Insects, spiders, pine seeds

Feeder Fare
Suet, sunflower seeds, suet/peanut butter spread

Pygmy

Brown-headed

Length: 4½ inches (11.5 cm), shorter than Black-capped Chickadee
Cap: brownish-gray on Pygmy; rich brown on Brown-headed
Eyeline: dusky
Cheek: white
Nape: whitish spot
Flanks: gray
Upperparts: bluish-gray
Underparts: buffy on Pygmy; paler on Brown-headed
Movement: any direction on tree trunks

Under Construction

Nesting in a tree cavity provides good protection for eggs and nestlings, but the excavation does take a lot of energy. It may take three to six weeks for a nuthatch to complete its nesting cavity, depending on factors such as how hard the wood is and the weather conditions. This is much longer than the time required to build a "regular" bird nest.

Brown Creeper
Certhia americana

ANOTHER BIRD SPECIES that hunts for food on tree trunks, the Brown Creeper usually forages by spiraling upward around the trunk. When it gets to the top, it flies down to the bottom of another trunk and repeats the process. Like a woodpecker, the Brown Creeper has very stiff tail feathers that it uses to prop itself against tree trunks. Its thin, curved beak is the perfect pair of tweezers for reaching into narrow cracks for insects and spiders.

Length: 5¼ inches (13.5 cm), similar to Black-capped Chickadee
Eyebrow: light
Beak: long, thin, curved
Upperparts: mottled brown
Wing: white bars and patches
Tail: long, stiff
Underparts: white
Movement: perches like a woodpecker on tree trunks

Natural Foods
Insects (adults and larvae), spiders, invertebrate eggs, sometimes seeds

Feeder Fare
Suet, suet/peanut butter spread, sometimes sunflower seeds

Bird Slumber Party
Some cavity-nesting birds — such as Eastern Bluebirds, Acorn Woodpeckers and Pygmy Nuthatches — may roost (sleep) together in an old woodpecker hole or nest box during the winter; the extra bodies help the group conserve heat and stay warm overnight. This photo shows Brown Creepers at a communal roosting site in a tree trunk that has been excavated by a Pileated Woodpecker. There are at least six birds in this pile!

Carolina Wren

(p. 190)

- White eyebrow
- Brown upperparts
- Orangey underparts

Bewick's Wren

(p. 191)

- White eyebrow
- Brown upperparts
- Gray underparts

Cactus Wren

(p. 192)

- White eyebrow
- Black breast spots
- White to orangey underparts

Hermit Thrush

(p. 195)

- Thin white eyering
- Dark breast spots
- Whitish underparts

Wrens, Kinglets and Thrushes

Kinglets and wrens are our some of our smallest backyard visitors, and many use feeders only rarely. Thrushes are bigger birds and some species are often spotted on the ground.

American Robin

(male) (p. 196)

- Broken, white eyering
- Yellow beak
- Grayish-brown upperparts
- Orange underparts

Varied Thrush

(male) (p. 197)

- Orange eyebrow
- Black breast band
- Orange wingbars
- Orange underparts

Eastern Bluebird

(male) (p. 194)

- Brilliant blue upperparts
- Orange throat and breast
- white belly and undertail coverts

Western Bluebird

(male) (p. 194)

- Brilliant blue upperparts and throat
- Orange breast and back
- Some blue on belly and undertail coverts

Ruby-crowned Kinglet (p. 193)

- Olive-brown overall
- Red crown on male
- White eyering
- White wingbars

Golden-crowned Kinglet (p. 193)

- Olive-brown overall
- Yellow cap with black border
- Orange central crown on male
- White wingbars

Carolina Wren
Thryothorus ludovicianus

"TEA KETTLE, TEA kettle, tea kettle, tea kettle!" This bubbly, loud and distinctive song might be the only way you know a Carolina Wren is around during the breeding season. This species is often quite shy and hard to see, but if you are able to entice one to a feeder, you can watch it all year long.

Natural Foods
Insects; spiders; wood lice; millipedes; snails; seeds and/or fruits of plants such as bayberry, poison ivy, sumac and sweet gum

Feeder Fare
Suet/peanut butter spread; hulled peanuts; possibly sunflower seeds, seed mixes, fruits

Length: 5½ inches (14 cm), similar to Black-capped Chickadee
Eyebrow: strong, white
Throat: white
Back: reddish-brown
Flanks: may be barred
Underparts: orangey
Wings, tail and undertail coverts: barred

Finding a Nest
Have you ever wondered where that little bird in your backyard has put its nest? Here is a tip for finding it: when you see a bird pick up nesting material, watch where it goes. Follow it to the spot where it disappeared, and then wait until it goes by again. You will get closer each time, until you can see where the nest is located. It is best not to get too close to the nest, however, especially during the building stage. Later on, you will be able to watch the adults bring food to their young! Remember to never disturb a bird's nest — it's the law.

Bewick's Wren

Thryomanes bewickii

THE BEWICK'S WREN has an interesting range history. It was a western bird that expanded into eastern North America when forest clearing provided them with their preferred open, scrubby habitat. Then, in the 1920s, House Wrens expanded into these eastern areas and seemed to outcompete the Bewick's Wrens, whose range contracted again.

Length: 5¼ inches (13.5 cm), similar to Black-capped Chickadee
Eyebrow: white or buffy
Throat: white
Upperparts: grayish or reddish-brown
Flanks: brown
Wing: some slight barring
Tail: long, thin, barred, white tips on outer edges
Underparts: gray
Undertail coverts: barred

Natural Foods
Insects, spiders, occasionally fruits and seeds

Feeder Fare
Suet, suet/peanut butter spread

Bird Song: An Auditory Fence

Bird song may sound pretty to us, but it is important business to birds. Besides attracting a mate, a male bird (who does most or all of the singing) uses his song to defend his territory from other males. He needs to defend his space to ensure that he has a nest site, hiding spots and enough food to support himself, his mate and his offspring. In essence, his song puts a fence around his territory, and males that cross it better watch out!

Cactus Wren

Campylorhynchus brunneicapillus

THIS BIRD IS well adapted to its desert home. For one thing, it never has to drink! It is able to get all of the moisture it needs from its food, though it may drink occasionally, when water is available. It forages in the shade when temperatures rise and, at 104ºF (40ºC) and above, will breathe with its beak open to cool itself by transferring heat through evaporation. Its domed nest also provides shade for its eggs and nestlings.

Length: 8½ inches (21.5 cm), similar to Red-winged Blackbird

Eyebrow: white

Eye: red

Breast: black spots

Flanks: light to dark rusty

Back: white streaks

Upperparts: brown

Wing and tail: barred

Underparts: white to orangey

Natural Foods

Insects; sometimes fruit and/or seeds of plants such as prickly pear, saguaro, elderberry, redberry, filaree, sumac and fiddle-neck

Feeder Fare

Suet, sunflower seeds, suet/peanut butter spread, peanuts, fruits

Spiny Shelter

Cactus Wrens live up to their name: their habitats are dominated by cactus and other spiny plants. With names like prickly pear, staghorn cholla, catclaw acacia and graythorn, these plants provide wrens with excellent protection from predators, including large mammals and raptors.

Ruby-crowned Kinglet and Golden-crowned Kinglet

Regulus calendula and *Regulus satrapa*

Male (*left*) and adult (*right*) Ruby-crowned Kinglet

Male (*left*) and female (*right*) Golden-crowned Kinglet

Length: 4-4 1/4 inches (10-11 cm)

RUBY-CROWNED KINGLET

Crown: bright red on male, can be concealed or raised; olive on female

Eyering: broken, white

Underparts: light olive

GOLDEN-CROWNED KINGLET

Cap: yellow with black border; orange central crown on male

Face: white eyebrow, black eyeline

Underparts: grayish

BOTH

Upperparts: olive

Wing: white wingbars, yellowish edges

Tail: yellowish edges on feathers

THESE REGAL BUT tiny birds are second only to hummingbirds on the list of our smallest backyard visitors. A Golden-crowned Kinglet may weigh less than two pennies! And yet, this species can survive winters as far north as Alaska! Ruby-crowned Kinglets are less cold hardy but are more likely to visit your bird feeder.

Natural Foods

Insects; spiders and their eggs; sometimes fruits and/or seeds of plants such as poison oak, cherry, wax myrtle, elderberry, red cedar, dogwood and persimmon

Feeder Fare

Suet, suet/peanut butter spread

Ruby-crowned Kinglet

Golden-crowned Kinglet

The King's Crown

Most of the time, you would be hard-pressed to see the red feathers on the top of a male Ruby-crowned Kinglet's head. But not so when he is singing! This little guy gives it his all and shows off his namesake head plumes. This tiny songster can also sing incredibly loudly for his size; he can be heard for almost a mile!

Eastern Bluebird and Western Bluebird

Sialia sialis and *Sialia mexicana*

Female Eastern Bluebird

Male Eastern Bluebird

"THE AIR THIS morning is full of bluebirds, and again it is spring." As Henry David Thoreau noted in 1851 (Thoreau, 1910), returning bluebirds are an indication of spring for many regions of North America. Their cheery calls and flashy blue feathers will brighten any early spring day. Why not attract a pair to your yard or local park? Check out the bird box information on pages 64–69.

Natural Foods

Insects; spiders; fruits of plants such as grape, dogwood, sumac, red cedar, bayberry, Virginia creeper, blueberry, serviceberry, thimbleberry, holly, hackberry, elderberry, pokeweed, mistletoe, cherry and currant

Eastern

Western

Feeder Fare

Dried fruits; mealworms; possibly some seed mixes, suet

Length: 7 inches (18 cm), similar to Downy Woodpecker

Throat: orange on male Eastern; duller on female Eastern; blue on male Western; gray on female Western

Neck: no orange on sides of Western

Breast: orange on male; duller on female

Back: orange sides on Western

Belly and undertail coverts: white on male Eastern; duller on female Eastern; some blue on male Western; gray on female Western

Upperparts: brilliant blue on male, grayish with blue highlights on female Juveniles are dark grayish-brown with whitish spots on breast and back and blue wing and tail feathers

Male (*left*) and female (*right*) Western Bluebird

Wing Wave

When you are this blue, why not show it off? Male bluebirds will sometimes perch and wave one or both wings when a female is nearby as part of their courtship display. This shows off more of the male's beautiful blue plumage. Once attracted, females sometimes wave with the males when they are together.

Hermit Thrush
Catharus guttatus

NORTH AMERICA HAS six species of similar-looking *Catharus* thrushes, but only the Hermit Thrush is a likely (though uncommon) feeder visitor. Its reddish tail helps distinguish it from other members of its genus. Often found on the ground, Hermit Thrushes can also be attracted to your yard with brush piles (see page 63), dense shrubs and a low water feature, such as a recirculating stream (see page 59).

Length: 6¾ inches (17 cm), similar to Downy Woodpecker
Eyering: thin
Moustache: dark
Breast: dark spots
Flank: grayish-brown
Upperparts: brown
Tail: reddish-brown
Underparts: whitish

Natural Foods
Insects; fruits (especially in winter) from plants such as holly, greenbrier, dogwood, sumac, grape, serviceberry, peppertree, poison oak, rose, viburnum and bittersweet

Feeder Fare
Possibly suet, suet/peanut butter spread, mealworms, dried fruits

Bird's Got Talent Winner!
Though less known than other songsters, the Hermit Thrush is often considered North America's most beautiful singer. This talent has given it other names, such as "swamp angel" and "nightingale of America." John Burroughs, an American naturalist of the late 1800s and early 1900s, describes the song well: "It realizes a peace and a deep solemn joy that only the finest souls may know" (in Studer, 1881).

American Robin

Turdus migratorius

Male

Female

Juvenile

THE AMERICAN ROBIN is probably the most identifiable small bird in North America. Populations have likely benefitted from residential lawns and the introduction of non-native earthworms, but this did come at a cost. Earthworms are resistant to DDT and concentrate it in their tissues. This caused massive die-offs of American Robins in the 1950s and alerted us to the dangers of these pesticides. So the next time you see a robin hopping across your lawn, remember our past environmental failures and hope for our future environmental successes.

Natural Foods

Insects; earthworms; fruits of plants such as cherry, dogwood, black gum, sumac, grape, red cedar, Virginia creeper, blackberry, hackberry, greenbrier, holly, persimmon, beautyberry, serviceberry, currant, peppertree, raspberry and apple

Feeder Fare

Possibly mealworms, fruits

Length: 10 inches (25.5 cm)
Eyering: broken, white
Beak: yellow on male; less yellow on female
Head: dark gray
Throat: some white on male; more white on female
Upperparts: gray on male; lighter and browner on female
Undertail coverts: white with grayish spots
Tail: white spots on corners
Underparts: orange on male; lighter orange on female
Juveniles are similar to females but have less orange and a spotted breast and back

Anting

I saw this American Robin acting strangely, so I snuck up to it for a closer look. It was anting! Many bird species have been known to lie down on an anthill and let the ants crawl over their feathers. It is thought that the formic acid in the ants may help repel the birds' external parasites. This robin was taking an even more active role in the anting process, running crushed ants through its feathers! Note the ant in its beak in this photo.

Varied Thrush

Ixoreus naevius

UNLIKE THE AMERICAN Robin, which favors a variety of habitats, the Varied Thrush prefers to breed in mature forests only. And while the cutting of these forests is obviously detrimental to this species, fragmentation of old-growth forests also causes population decreases. When forests are fragmented into smaller plots, it creates more forest edges, which increases nest predation. One study showed that Varied Thrush nests within 80 feet (25 m) of the forest edge were twice as likely to be destroyed by a predator than nests that were 330 feet (100 m) or more from the forest edge. This shows that sometimes it isn't just the amount of forest cover, but it is the size and continuity of the forest cover that is important.

Male

Female

Natural Foods

Insects; millipedes; centipedes; snails; acorns; fruits and/or seeds of plants such as snowberry, raspberry, honeysuckle, apple, prune, huckleberry, thimbleberry, salmonberry, dogwood, ash and blueberry

Feeder Fare

Possibly seed mixes, fruits, mealworms, suet, suet/peanut butter spread

Length: 9½ inches (24 cm), slightly shorter than American Robin

Eyebrow: thick, orange

Breast: thick black band on male; less distinct band on female

Upperparts: dark gray on male; lighter and browner on female

Wing: orange bars and flight feather edges

Underparts: orange on male; lighter orange on female

Flanks: gray

Undertail coverts: white with grayish spots

This May Leave You Scratching Your Head . . .

Birds can only preen their head with their feet. Some species bring their foot over their wing to scratch their head (as shown here), while others bring their foot under their wing. Some species even start, as youngsters, to scratch their head under their wing and then gradually change to scratching over their wing! Which way do your birds scratch their head?

Gray Catbird

(p. 200)

- Black cap
- Gray body
- Rufous undertail coverts

Northern Mockingbird (p. 201)

- Dark eyeline
- Light gray upperparts
- White wingbars
- White underparts

Brown Thrasher

(p. 202)

- Dark breast streaks
- Brown upperparts
- White wingbars
- White underparts

Curve-billed Thrasher

(p. 203)

- Curved beak
- Faint spots on breast
- Gray or brownish upperparts
- Faint wingbars

Mimics, Starlings and Waxwings

Mimics (which include thrashers, mockingbirds and catbirds) are songsters that repeat other birds' songs. All mimics have long beaks and long tails. Starlings are introduced birds that can also mimic other birds' songs. They have very pointy beaks and short tails. Waxwings are social fruit eaters that have thin voices and short crests. They also have beautifully colored markings, including waxy red tips on some of their secondary feathers.

European Starling (summer) (p. 204)
- All black with iridescent purple and green
- Straight yellow beak

European Starling (winter) (p. 204)
- All black with light spots
- Straight dark beak

Cedar Waxwing (p. 205)
- Crest
- Black mask
- Yellow-tipped tail
- Yellow underparts

Bohemian Waxwing (p. 205)
- Crest
- Black mask
- Yellow stripe on wings
- Yellow-tipped tail

Gray Catbird

Dumetella carolinensis

THE CALL OF this bird gave it its name. Jacob Studer wrote, "In spring or summer, when approaching thickets of brambles, the first salutation you receive is from the Cat Bird. One unacquainted with his notes would conclude that some vagrant kitten had got bewildered among the briers and was in want of assistance, so exactly alike is the call of this bird to the cry of that animal" (1881).

Length: 8½ inches (21.5 cm), similar to Red-winged Blackbird
All gray
Cap and tail: black
Undertail coverts: rufous

Natural Foods

Insects; spiders; fruits from plants such as blackberry, cherry, elderberry, greenbrier, grape, sumac, blueberry, pokeweed, dogwood, serviceberry, sassafras, bayberry, holly, poison ivy, beautyberry and mulberry

Feeder Fare

Fruits, mealworms, suet, jelly, raisins soaked in water, suet/peanut butter spread, sugar water

Copy Catbird

Most birds have distinctive songs that they use to claim their territory or to attract a mate. Not so for birds in the family Mimidae, the mimics. These include catbirds, thrashers and mockingbirds. As their name suggests, this group copies other birds' songs and other sounds to impress potential mates. Some mimics have over 200 song types in their repertoire! Listen to your backyard mockingbird, thrasher or catbird — how many different sounds can you count?

Northern Mockingbird

Mimus polyglottos

"THE SWEETER NOTES of Nature's own music." So wrote John James Audubon in the 1830s (Audubon, 1999), describing the song of this favorite North American bird. As the male gets older, he may add more and more song types to his abilities, and this likely makes him more desirable as a mate. Studies suggest that mockingbirds mostly use song to attract mates rather than to defend territories.

Natural Foods

Insects; spiders; plants such as holly, greenbrier, pokeweed, Virginia creeper, red cedar, elderberry, blackberry, black gum, grape, hackberry, mulberry, beautyberry, bluewood, peppertree and poison oak

Feeder Fare

Suet/peanut butter spread, mealworms, fruits, sunflower seeds, suet, sugar water

Length: 10 inches (25.5 cm), similar to American Robin
Eyeline: dark
Eye: yellowish
Wing: white wingbars, with white flash that is very apparent when wings are spread
Upperparts: gray
Tail: long with white outer feathers
Underparts: white to buffy

Lots to Learn: Wing Flash

Have you seen a Northern Mockingbird flash its wings? It is very common behavior for this species, but we still don't know why they do it. Suggestions include territorial displays, chasing away potential nest predators or startling insect prey out into the open. Even some of our most familiar birds have mysteries that biologists still haven't figured out.

Brown Thrasher

Toxostoma rufum

TELLING MIMICS APART when you can hear them but not see them can be challenging. In the east, things are a little easier because there are only three main contenders: the Northern Mockingbird, the Brown Thrasher and the Gray Catbird. Often you can tell these singers apart because the mockingbird is the most talented, the thrasher usually sings each phrase in pairs and the catbird may have a whiny "mew" among its warbled notes. If you can learn to identify your backyard birds by their songs, you will enjoy them even more.

Natural Foods
Insects; spiders; small frogs; small salamanders; small lizards; acorns; fruits and/or seeds of plants such as blackberry, cherry, elderberry, corn, dogwood, black gum, Virginia creeper, bayberry, blueberry, sumac, pine, holly, grape, viburnum, hackberry and mulberry

Feeder Fare
Seed mixes, suet/peanut butter spread, cracked corn, suet, mealworms, fruits

Length: 11½ inches (29 cm), similar to Blue Jay and Steller's Jay
Eyes: yellow
Face: grayish
Breast: dark streaks
Upperparts: reddish-brown
Wings: white wingbars
Tail: long, pale tips on outer feathers
Underparts: white

Defense!
Defending one's eggs or young from predators is a risky business for birds. The predator can often be a threat to the parent, too, so some birds stay quiet, hoping the predator won't find their nest. Others — such as thrashers, mockingbirds, orioles and Red-winged Blackbirds — actively defend their nest. Here, a Brown Thrasher is trying to keep a snake from getting too close to its nestlings.

Curve-billed Thrasher

Toxostoma curvirostre

THE CURVE-BILLED Thrasher is well named, although some other thrasher species have beaks that are even more curved. In fact, the genus name for seven of our North American thrashers is Toxostoma, which means "arched mouth." Thrashers use this formidable tool to sweep, probe and dig through leaf litter and soil when looking for food.

Length: 11 inches (28 cm), similar to Blue Jay and Steller's Jay
Eye: yellow to orange
Breast: variable blurry spotting, most distinctive in Texas population
Upperparts: grayish-brown
Underparts: lighter
Wing: faint wingbars
Tail: long with pale tips on outer feathers

Natural Foods

Insects; spiders; millipedes; fruits and/or seeds of plants such as prickly pear, saguaro, wheat, corn, bluewood, barley and hackberry

Feeder Fare

Seed mixes, suet/peanut butter spread, cracked corn, suet, mealworms, fruits

Catching a Few Rays

At some point you may look into your backyard and see a bird in the same strange position this Curve-billed Thrasher is in. This bird is sunning itself. Birds likely sun themselves to keep their feathers healthy — it makes external parasites move around so they are easier to remove during preening. It could also be connected to vitamin D production or getting warmth from the sun. Whatever the reason, it's fun to see the strange positions that some birds put themselves in when catching a few rays.

European Starling

Sturnus vulgaris

IN 1890–91, APPROXIMATELY 100 European Starlings were released in New York City. We now have over 200 million of them, and they range from the Atlantic coast to the Pacific, and from Alaska and Nunavut south to Mexico. Starlings achieved this amazing population increase and range expansion by being very adaptable and able to eat a wide variety of foods.

Summer adult

Natural Foods

Insects; spiders; earthworms; snails; millipedes; fruits of plants such as cherry, sumac, mulberry, bayberry, elderberry, apple, black gum, sumac and poison ivy; human garbage

Winter adult

Feeder Fare

Suet, suet/peanut butter spread, corn, peanuts, mixed seed, wheat, milo, sugar water, mealworms

Length: 8½ inches (21.5 cm), similar to Red-winged Blackbird
All black with purplish or greenish iridescence in summer; light spotting overall in winter
Beak: long, pointed; yellow in summer; dark in winter
Wing and tail: brown edges on feathers
Legs: pinkish
Juveniles are light brown overall and have a light throat

Squatter Supreme

European Starlings have been competing with native birds for cavity nesting sites ever since they arrived in North America. And size is no object: there are cases of them fighting over cavities with birds from the size of Tree Swallows and Eastern Bluebirds up to Wood Ducks and Buffleheads. They have even been known to evict woodpeckers that have just finished drilling a nest cavity. Here, a Red-headed Woodpecker tries to defend its nest from a starling.

Molting from juvenile coloration to winter coloration

Juvenile

Bohemian Waxwing and Cedar Waxwing

Bombycilla garrulus and *Bombycilla cedrorum*

Bohemian

Adult Cedar

Juvenile Cedar

THESE BEAUTIFUL, SATINY birds are backyard favorites — when they visit. Waxwings are known for moving around quite a bit when looking for food, so they are not consistent visitors. As well, they are usually more interested in your fruiting trees and shrubs than your feeder, so keep that in mind when choosing backyard woody plants!

Natural Foods

Fruits from plants such as peppertree, cherry, grape, gooseberry, strawberry, mistletoe, apple, hawthorn, blackberry, red cedar, dogwood, hackberry, chokeberry, mulberry, serviceberry, viburnum, pokeweed, mountain ash and elderberry

Bohemian Waxwing

Cedar Waxwing

Feeder Fare

Fruits, jellies

Length:
Cedar: 7¼ inches (18.5 cm), similar to Brown-headed Cowbird
Bohemian: 8¼ inches (21 cm), shorter than Red-winged Blackbird
Cedar is brown overall; Bohemian is grayer overall
Crest
Mask: black bordered with white
Moustache: white
Throat: black
Belly: yellowish on Cedar; no yellow on Bohemian
Wing: grayish; white and yellow flashes on Bohemian
Secondary feathers: red "drops" on ends
Rump: grayish
Tail: grayish with yellow tip
Undertail coverts: white on Cedar; chestnut on Bohemian
Juveniles have more white on face and belly, blurry streaks on breast and no red on secondary feathers; Cedar has less yellow on belly, and Bohemian has less gray on belly

Could I Have This Dance?

Cedar Waxwings do a dance called the "side hop." This courtship behavior starts when the male brings a food gift to a female and passes it to her. She then does one hop away and then hops back and passes the gift back to the male. He then hops away and hops back, and the display repeats, often terminating when the female finally eats the gift!

House Finch

(male) (p. 213)

- Red eyebrow
- Red throat and breast
- Brown streaks on flanks

Purple Finch

(male) (p. 214)

- Raspberry-red head
- Raspberry-red throat and breast
- Raspberry-red on back
- Indistinct streaks on flanks

Cassin's Finch

(male) (p. 215)

- Head is often peaked
- Raspberry-red crown
- Raspberry-red throat and breast
- Faint raspberry-red on back
- Indistinct, fine streaks on flanks

Pine Grosbeak

(male) (p. 212)

- Reddish-pink head
- Large beak
- Reddish-pink breast
- White wingbars
- Gray belly

Fantastic Finches

The males of these small seed eaters are well known for their musical songs and brilliant plumage. Finches are often found in flocks, especially in winter, and are commonly attracted to bird feeders.

Red Crossbill

(male) (p. 216)

• Orangish-red overall
• Crossed beak
• Dark wings

White-winged Crossbill

(male) (p. 216)

• Pink overall
• Crossed beak
• Dark wing
• White wingbars

Common Redpoll

(male) (p. 220)

• Red forehead
• Yellow beak
• Black face
• Pink breast
• Streaks on upperparts and flanks
• White wingbars

Evening Grosbeak

(male) (p. 217)

• Yellow forehead and eyebrow
• Large, pale beak
• Brown head and upperparts
• Black wing
• White wing patches
• Yellowish underparts

American Goldfinch

(summer male) (p. 218)

• Yellow overall
• Black cap
• Orange beak
• Black wing
• White wingbars

Lesser Goldfinch

(male, green-backed form) (p. 219)

• Black cap
• Dark beak
• Green back
• Black wing
• White wingbars
• Yellow underparts

Lesser Goldfinch

(male, black-backed form) (p. 219)

• Dark beak
• Black upperparts
• White wingbars
• Yellow underparts

Lawrence's Goldfinch

(male) (p. 219)

• Gray overall
• Light beak
• Black face
• Yellow breast patch
• Black wing with gold highlights

House Finch

(female) (p. 213)

- Plain face
- Brown upperparts
- Breast streaks
- Dirty-white underparts

Purple Finch

(female) (p. 214)

- White eyebrow
- Brown upperparts
- Dark breast streaks
- White underparts

Cassin's Finch

(female) (p. 215)

- Faint eyebrow
- Thin white eyering
- Brown upperparts
- Dark breast streaks
- White underparts

Pine Siskin

(p. 221)

- Brown upperparts
- Streaked breast
- Pale wingbars (yellower on males)

Black Rosy-Finch

(p. 211)

- Blackish overall
- Gray hind crown and eyebrow
- Pinkish wing

Gray-crowned Rosy-Finch (p. 211)

- Brownish overall
- Gray hind crown and eyebrow; some have gray cheek
- Black face
- Pinkish wing

Brown-capped Rosy-Finch (p. 211)

- Brownish overall
- Some gray in hind crown
- Black face
- Pinkish wing

American Goldfinch

(winter) (p. 218)

- Brownish-olive overall
- May have yellow wash on throat
- Dusky wing
- Pale wingbars

Fantastic Finches

Female finches are often duller than males and can be hard to tell apart from some sparrows. Rosy-Finches are western birds with pinkish washes to their feathers. The House Sparrow is an introduced Old World sparrow that is not closely related to our North American sparrows, even though it looks very similar.

Red Crossbill

(female) (p. 216)

- Brownish-olive overall
- Crossed beak
- Dark, plain wings

White-winged Crossbill

(female) (p. 216)

- Brownish-olive overall
- Streaks on body
- Crossed beak
- Dark wings
- White wingbars

Common Redpoll

(female) (p. 220)

- Red forehead
- Yellow beak
- Black face
- Whitish breast
- Streaked upperparts and flanks
- White wingbars

Hoary Redpoll

(p. 220)

- Red forehead
- Stubbier beak than Common Redpoll
- Black face
- Whitish breast
- Plain or streaked flanks
- White wingbars
- Streaked upperparts

Pine Grosbeak

(female) (p. 212)

- Gray overall
- Olive or rufous head
- Short beak
- White wingbars

Evening Grosbeak

(female) (p. 217)

- Gray overall
- Large, pale beak
- Dusky lore
- Yellow wash on neck
- Black wing
- White wing patch

House Sparrow

(male) (p. 210)

- Gray crown
- Black mask
- Black throat and breast
- Brown upperparts
- White wingbar
- Gray underparts

House Sparrow

(female) (p. 210)

- Light eyebrow
- Black throat and breast
- Brown upperparts
- Gray underparts

House Sparrow

Passer domesticus

Summer male

Winter male

Female

THE HOUSE SPARROW might be the most disliked bird in North America, but we must always keep in mind that we brought it here from Europe. One hundred House Sparrows were released in Brooklyn, New York, in 1851. They are now found across the continent and have quite an impressive worldwide distribution. While House Sparrows can be destructive to native wildlife, we are more so. And both humans and House Sparrows are here to stay, so it is time to enjoy these guys at our feeders while also doing what we can to help nature keep everything in balance.

Natural Foods

Oats, corn, wheat, ragweed, crabgrass, knotweed, bristle grass

Feeder Fare

Seed mixes, millet, cracked corn, sunflower seeds, suet/peanut butter spread, sugar water

Length: 6¼ inches (16 cm), similar to Dark-eyed Junco

MALE

Crown: gray

Beak: black in summer; pale yellow in winter

Face, chin and breast: black in summer; less black on face and breast in winter

Cheek, side, belly and undertail coverts: grayish-white

Upperparts: rich brown in summer; duller in winter

Back: streaked

Wing: white wingbars

Underparts: gray

FEMALE

Head and body: grayish-brown

Eyebrow: buffy

Beak: pale

Throat and breast: black

Back: streaked

Upperparts: brown

Wing: thin wingbars

Underparts: gray

Streetwise

House Sparrows do well when living with their best friends: us. They make themselves at home in cityscapes by stealing food from restaurant patios, warming up beside bright streetlights and nesting in holes and cracks in buildings, poles and signs. Some sparrows have even figured out that if they fly in front of motion-detector sensors, the doors will open and allow them into shopping center food courts!

Gray-crowned Rosy-Finch, Black Rosy-Finch and Brown-capped Rosy-Finch

Leucosticte tephrocotis, Leucosticte atrata and *Leucosticte australis*

ROSY-FINCHES ARE mountain birds that live in remote areas. When they visit lower altitude feeders in the winter, they are surprisingly tame and may let you approach them quite closely. This is a gift since it will allow you to get a great look at their pink highlights!

Natural Foods

Many seeds, including Lewisia, oats, knotweed, chickweed, pine, wheat, peppergrass, sedge, timothy, cinquefoil, grama grass, pigweed, love grass, rush, thistle, mustard and crowberry; insects and spiders in summer

Feeder Fare

Sunflower seeds, seed mixes, millet, cracked corn

Length: 6¼ inches (16 cm), similar to Dark-eyed Junco

Head: gray

Forehead: black

Crown: gray, brownish on Brown-capped

Cheeks: brown on "interior" Gray-crowned and Brown-capped; blackish on Black

Throat: dark

Body: rich brown with pinkish highlights on male; duller overall on female; blackish on Black

Wing: pinkish

"Interior" (*left*), "Coastal" (*right*) Gray-crowned Rosy-Finch   Black Rosy-Finch   Brown-capped Rosy-Finch

Gray-crowned Rosy-Finch   Black Rosy-Finch   Brown-capped Rosy-Finch

Winter Roosting

Living on the tops of mountains has helped these birds evolve some great cold-temperature survival strategies. One is roosting (sleeping) in protected places during the winter. By getting out of the wind, the birds save a lot of heat energy. Rosy-Finch flocks may roost in wells, caves, buildings, mine shafts and, as shown here, old Cliff Swallow nests!

Pine Grosbeak

Pinicola enucleator

Adult male

Adult female

Russet first-year male or adult female

THE STRIKING MALE Pine Grosbeak is a sight to behold against newly fallen snow. In 1851, Henry David Thoreau called them "magnificent winter birds . . . with red or crimson reflections more beautiful than a steady bright red would be" (Thoreau, 1910). This large finch can be quite tame and allow you to get quite close, giving you a good view.

Natural Foods

Seeds, buds and/or fruits of plants such as pine, blackberry, red cedar, mountain ash, snowberry, willow, honeysuckle, maple, ash, grape, dogwood, elm, poplar, crabapple and crowberry; some insects in summer

Feeder Fare

Sunflower seeds, possibly suet, seed mixes, fruits

Length: 9 inches (23 cm), similar to Red-winged Blackbird

Eyeline: short, dark

Head: bright reddish-pink on male; olive on female

Throat: gray on female

Breast and side: bright reddish-red on male; gray on female

Rump: bright reddish-red on male; olive on female

Back: streaked

Wings: white wingbars

Belly and undertail coverts: gray

First-winter female is duller overall

First-year male and russet adult female are similar to adult female, except for rusty coloring replaces the olive coloring

Irruptions

Some bird populations have "irruption years"; these are winters during which southern feeder watchers get to see some northern bird species that rarely visit southern areas. Some examples are Bohemian Waxwings, Pine Grosbeaks and redpolls. Many people think that the birds fly south because of the cold, but it is actually because their food supply is depleted, which prompts them to move to a place that has the food they need. Pine Grosbeaks, for example, may irrupt south when mountain ashes don't have a good fruit production year.

House Finch

Haemorhous mexicanus

ONCE ONLY A western bird, the House Finch is now found across the continent, after several illegally kept "Hollywood finches" were released on Long Island, New York, in 1940. They are now equally at home in eastern subdivisions and southwestern deserts. They are also not shy about being around humans and often nest in front yard spruces, hanging flower baskets or even wreaths on front doors.

Natural Foods

Seeds and fruits of plants such as filaree, turkey mullein, knotweed, prune, fig, mustard, pigweed, thistle, chickweed, wild raisin and tarweed

Feeder Fare

Sunflower seeds, seed mixes, safflower, nyjer, corn, suet, fruit, sugar water, possibly millet

Length: 6 inches (15 cm), similar to Dark-eyed Junco

ADULT MALE

Brown overall

Forehead, eyebrow, breast and rump: red on most, orange or yellow on some

Beak: short, rounded

Belly, sides and undertail coverts: whitish

Lower breast and sides: brown streaks

Back: streaked

Wing: whitish wingbars

ADULT FEMALE AND FIRST-YEAR MALE

Beak: short, rounded

Head and upperparts: brown

Breast and side: brown streaks

Back: streaked

Wing: whitish wingbars

Underparts: dirty white

Color Variant

Birds get their yellow, orange and red colors from carotenoid pigments found in their diet. Most male House Finches have red foreheads, breasts and rumps, but you may sometimes see orange or even yellow instead. These variations depend on the amounts and types of carotenoids that the birds eat. And because the birds molt every year, a male that is red one year could end up yellow or orange the next year!

Purple Finch

Haemorhous purpureus

Adult male

Female or first-year male

IN 1847, HENRY David Thoreau wrote of the Purple Finch: "It has the crimson hues of the October evenings, and its plumage still shines as if it had caught and preserved some of their tints (beams?). Many a serene evening lies snugly packed under its wing" (Thoreau, 1910). This brilliant finch has also been described as being dipped in raspberry juice.

Natural Foods

Fruits, seeds and/or buds of plants such as elm, tulip tree, apple, peach, cherry, pear, red cedar, sycamore, maple, ragweed, aspen, dogwood, sweet gum, honeysuckle, cocklebur and ash

Feeder Fare

Sunflower seeds, seed mixes, fruits, peanuts, millet, cracked corn, nyjer, possibly safflower seeds

Length: 6 inches (15 cm), similar to Dark-Eyed Junco

ADULT MALE

Cheek: brownish

Head, breast, side and rump: raspberry-red

Belly and undertail coverts: white

Back: reddish wash with brown streaks

Flank: faint to distinct brown streaks

Wing: reddish wash with reddish wingbars

ADULT FEMALE AND FIRST-YEAR MALE

Eyebrow and throat: white

Head: brown

Throat, breast and sides: dark streaks

Back: streaked

Upperparts: brown

Wing: thin white wingbars

Underparts: white

Dance for Romance

Male Purple Finches know how to attract a mate: dance! They fluff out their feathers, spread their wings and hop around a female. Sometimes one may even carry a piece of nesting material in his beak to really get the point across.

Cassin's Finch

Haemorhous cassinii

Male

Female or first-year male

JUST LIKE HIS close relatives, the Purple Finch and the House Finch, the male Cassin's Finch is an accomplished singer of beautiful and fluid warbles. But unlike his relatives, the Cassin's Finch may mimic the song or call phrases of other birds and add them to his song.

Natural Foods

Fruits, buds and/or seeds of plants such as pine, manzanita, poplar, cotoneaster and mulberry; some insects in summer

Feeder Fare

Sunflower seeds, cracked corn, nyjer, possibly millet

Length: 6¼ inches (16 cm), similar to Dark-eyed Junco

ADULT MALE

Cheek: brownish

Head, breast, side and rump: raspberry-red

Belly: white

Flank: faint, thin brown streaks

Back: pinkish wash with brown streaks

Undertail coverts: white with faint, thin brown streaks

Wing: pinkish wash with pinkish wingbars

ADULT FEMALE AND FIRST-YEAR MALE

Eyebrow: indistinct, thin, white

Eyering: thin, white

Head: brown

Throat, breast and sides: dark streaks

Back: streaked

Upperparts: brown

Wing: thin white wingbars

Underparts: white

Finch Faces

House Finches (*bottom*), Purple Finches (*top*) and Cassin's Finches (*center*) can be challenging to identify. This chart outlines some of the distinct features of the heads of these birds, which should help you tell them apart.

Head shape: rounded or slight peak
Beak shape: conical with straight top
Head color: male: red wash overall, female: distinctive light eyebrow

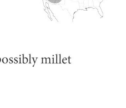

Head shape: peaked
Beak shape: long, conical with straight top
Head color: male: red brightest on cap, female: thin eyebrow and eyering

Head shape: rounded
Beak shape: short and rounded on top
Head color: male: red eyebrow, female: plain face

Red Crossbill and White-winged Crossbill

Loxia curvirostra and *Loxia leucoptera*

Male (*left*), first-year male (*center*) and female (*right*) Red

Male (*left*), first-year male (*center*) and female (*right*) White-winged

Length: 6¼ –6½ inches (16–16.5 cm), similar to Dark-eyed Junco

RED CROSSBILL

Beak: crossed

Body: dull red on adult male; dull orange on first-year male; olive-yellow or olive-gray on female

Wing and tail: dark

Undertail coverts: whitish

WHITE-WINGED CROSSBILL

Beak: crossed

Body: pink (redder in summer) on adult male; orange on first-year male; brownish-gray and streaked on female

Breast: olive-yellow wash with blurry streaks on female

Side: grayish

Rump: olive-yellow wash on female

Wing: black with bold white wingbars on adult male; brownish on first-year male and female

Tail: black or brownish

Undertail coverts: whitish

CROSSBILLS ARE THE parrots of the songbird world. In 1860, Henry David Thoreau wrote that Red Crossbills "were very parrot-like both in color (especially the male, greenish and orange, etc.) and in their manner of feeding — holding the hemlock cones in one claw and rapidly extracting the seeds with their bills, thus trying one cone after another very fast" (Thoreau, 1910). They use their crossed beaks to spread apart the scales of unopened conifer cones so they can get their tongue inside and pull out a seed.

Natural Foods

Seeds of plants such as spruce, pine, hemlock, tamarack, fir, birch, alder, red cedar, cottonwood and maple; some insects in summer

Feeder Fare

Sunflower seeds, safflower seeds

Red Crossbill

White-winged Crossbill

Are You a Leftie?

Crossbills could be considered righties or lefties. If their lower mandible curves to the left side of the upper mandible, they usually hold the cone they are feeding on with their right foot. If their lower mandible curves to the right, they use their left foot. This likely makes their foraging technique as efficient as possible.

Evening Grosbeak
Coccothraustes vespertinus

Male

Female

LIKE THE AMERICAN Goldfinch, the male Evening Grosbeak's yellow plumage is bold and beautiful. But, unlike the goldfinch, he keeps his color all year long. The female, too, is a striking bird, with muted splashes of color. This grosbeak's feeding habits are legendary. As Brunton notes, "The Evening Grosbeak's seemingly inexhaustible appetite for sunflower seeds at winter feeders caused the late John Bird to con a graphic nickname for them in the mid-1960s: he called them 'Greedies'" (in McNicholl and Cranmer-Byng, 1994).

Natural Foods
Seeds and/or fruits of plants such as dogwood, maple, cherry, mountain ash, pine, cedar, hackberry, snowberry and serviceberry; insects in summer

Feeder Fare
Sunflower seeds

Length: 8 inches (20.5 cm), larger than Brown-headed Cowbird
ADULT MALE
Eyebrow and forehead: yellow
Beak: pale
Head to lower back and belly: dark brown blending to yellow
Wing: black with large white patch
Tail: black
ADULT FEMALE
Lore: dusky
Head and body: grayish
Side and nape: yellowish wash
Wing: black with gray and white patches
Tail: black with white spots
Undertail coverts: white

Sugar-bird
This species wasn't common in the eastern part of North America until the late 1800s. Some attribute the extension of its range to the planting of Manitoba Maples, whose seeds are another of the Evening Grosbeak's favorites. In 1921, Percy Taverner called this planting a "baited highway" since it encouraged this species to follow the trees (in Bent, 1968). Because Evening Grosbeaks like maple buds, maple keys and even maple sap, one of their first names was "Sugar-bird."

American Goldfinch

Spinus tristis

Summer male (*left*) and female (*right*)

Winter (*left*) and molting male (*right*)

Length: 5 inches (13 cm), similar to Black-capped Chickadee

SUMMER MALE

Head and body: bright yellow

Forehead: black

Beak: orange

Wing: black with white wingbar

Tail: black with extensive white spots

Undertail coverts: white

Rump: white

SUMMER FEMALE AND WINTER

Beak: pinkish-orange on summer female; dusky on winter

Throat: yellowish on summer female and winter adult male

Shoulder: yellow patch on winter adult male (may be concealed)

Upperparts: olive-green on summer female; brownish-gray on winter

Wing: black with white or buffy wingbar on male; dark brownish-black with wingbar on female

Tail: black with whitish spots on male; dark brownish-black with spots on female

Undertail coverts: white

Breast and belly: yellowish-olive on summer female; grayish on winter

First-winter male and winter female are duller and browner overall

IT IS TRULY a joy to have American Goldfinches with us, and many North Americans can enjoy them throughout the year. For many of us, however, the birds we have in the summer migrate south, and the ones we have in the winter are from farther north. American Goldfinches often nest in suburban areas, so we can watch their entire life cycle right in our own backyards.

Natural Foods

Seeds of "weeds," annual and perennial plants, alder, birch, white cedar, elm; insects (very few)

Feeder Fare

Sunflower seeds, nyjer

Successful Seedy Strategy

American Goldfinches are one of our latest breeding birds, likely because they delay their nesting season to coincide with the production of thistle seeds. Because they can raise their young on a diet of strictly seeds, they can't raise Brown-headed Cowbird chicks (see page 259). Any cowbird nestling that hatches in a goldfinch nest eventually dies since it doesn't get enough protein from the seeds to grow feathers; most other birds, even seed-eaters, feed their nestlings at least some insects. The goldfinch's own nestlings are able to get the protein they need for feather growth from seeds alone.

Lesser Goldfinch and Lawrence's Goldfinch

Spinus psaltria and Spinus lawrencei

Male "Western" (*left*), "Texas" (*center*) and female (*right*) Lesser Goldfinch

Male (*left*) and female (*right*) Lawrence's Goldfinch

WHILE THE AMERICAN Goldfinch ranges widely over southern Canada and the lower 48 states, these two smaller goldfinch species have a much more restricted range. Lucky California and Arizona get to have all three at once! When they are found together at a feeder, the Lesser Goldfinches usually dominate the Lawrence's, even though they are smaller.

Natural Foods
Seeds of plants such as star thistle, pigweed, turkey mullein, tarweed, chamise and chickweed

Feeder Fare
Sunflower seeds, nyjer

Pondering the Poop
Songbirds are usually quite fastidious about removing their young's feces when they are in the nest. But when the young get close to fledgling (leaving the nest), the parents stop removing the feces, and the chicks just poop over the side of the nest. If you find an empty nest that has lots of bird poop around the edges, there is a good chance that the parents were successful in raising the young to fledging. Empty nests with no poop might indicate that a predator got there first. This photo shows some Lesser Goldfinch chicks almost ready to leave the nest. See the poop?

LESSER
Length: 4½ inches (11.5 cm), smaller than Black-capped Chickadee
Cap: black on male
Upperparts: greenish on "Western" male; black on "Texas" male; duller overall on female
Wing: pale wingbars and patch on "Western"; white wingbar and patch on "Texas"
Underparts: yellow on male
Female is duller overall.

LAWRENCE'S
Length: 4¾ inches (12 cm), smaller than Black-capped Chickadee
Forehead, face and throat: black
Face: black on male; gray on female
Beak: pinkish
Body: gray
Breast: yellow patch
Wing: black with yellow patches
Female is brownish-gray overall, with less yellow

Lesser Goldfinch   Lawrence's Goldfinch

Common Redpoll and Hoary Redpoll

Acanthis flammea and *Acanthis hornemanni*

Male Common Redpoll

Likely a female Common Redpoll

Likely a male Hoary Redpoll

EVERYONE WITH A bird feeder that has been visited by redpolls waits each year for them to return. The pink of the males seems to glow. In 1855, Henry David Thoreau wrote, "What a rich contrast! Tropical colors, crimson breasts on cold white snow! Such etherealness, such delicacy in their forms, such ripeness in their colors, in this stern and barren season!" (Thoreau, 1910). And even though they look delicate, they can survive severe winter conditions. To do this, they may have to eat more than 40 percent of their body weight in seeds per day.

Natural Foods

Seeds of plants such as ragweed, alder, birch, goosefoot, smartweed, pigweed, bristle grass and timothy

Feeder Fare

Sunflower seeds, nyjer

"Southern" Common

"Greater" Common

"Southern" Hoary

"Hornemann's" Hoary

Four Subspecies

The descriptions above are for the subspecies of this complex group of birds that backyard birders are most likely to see (the "southern" ones). The Greenland, or Greater, subspecies of the Common Redpoll is rarer in North America and is larger, browner and darker overall. The Hornemann's subspecies of the Hoary Redpoll is rarer in North America and is larger and whiter overall. Keen birders should watch for these rarer subspecies mixed in with large redpoll flocks.

Length: 5¼ –5½ inches (13–14 cm), similar to Black-capped Chickadee

Forecrown: red on male; smaller on female

Face and chin: black

Beak: stubby and short on Hoary, giving it a "pushed-in" face

Breast: variable bright pink wash on Common; lighter pink on Hoary; little or no pink on females

Back: streaked

Side: dark streaks on male and adult female Common; slight brown wash on first-year female; thin, faint streaks on HOARY

Wing: white wingbars

Rump: variable bright pink wash, usually streaked on Common; white, usually no streaks on Hoary

Underparts: white

Undertail coverts: thin streaks on Common; usually none on Hoary

Male Hoary has less streaking and is whiter overall

First-year female Hoary may have slight brownish wash

Common Redpoll

Hoary Redpoll

Pine Siskin
Spinus pinus

Male

Likely a female

THIS SMALL FINCH can be very tame, especially if it gets used to a bird feeder. In some cases, they may even land on you. The siskins coming to E.R. Davis's feeder in 1926 became even bolder than that: "In a short time the siskins discovered this opening in a window pane, and one after another would come right into my kitchen. Now and then some members would elect to spend the night in the warm room, sleeping on the clothes-line" (in Bent, 1968). Talk about making yourself at home!

Length: 5 inches (13 cm), similar to Black-capped Chickadee
Beak: thin, pointy
Breast, sides and undertail coverts: dark streaks
Upperparts: brownish streaks
Wing: yellowish to white wingbar, bright yellow stripe seen in flight on male; white wingbar and less yellow on female
Tail: some yellow in male; less yellow in female
Underparts: white

Natural Foods

Seeds of plants such as filaree, pine, alder, star thistle, eucalyptus, sunflower, birch, white cedar, hemlock, tamarack, spruce, chickweed, elm, maple and red cedar; occasionally insects; occasionally spiders

Feeder Fare

Sunflower seeds, nyjer, possibly suet

Flock Fighting

Pine Siskins are pretty confident for their tiny size. They regularly dominate larger Purple Finches at feeders and will even try to push around much larger Evening Grosbeaks. They also quite often fight among themselves. They use noncontact displays first, such as lunges and spread wings and tails. If that doesn't work, then physical fights may occur.

Yellow-rumped "Myrtle" Warbler
(summer male) (p. 226)
- White throat
- Black mask
- Yellow rump and side patches
- White underparts

Yellow-rumped "Myrtle" Warbler
(winter) (p. 226)
- White throat
- Brown upperparts
- Yellow rump and side patches
- Whitish underparts

Yellow-rumped "Audubon's" Warbler
(summer male) (p. 226)
- Yellow throat
- Black mask
- Yellow rump and side patches
- White underparts

Yellow-rumped "Audubon's" Warbler
(winter) (p. 226)
- Yellow throat
- Brown upperparts
- Yellow rump and side patches
- White underparts

Winning Warblers

Most of our Canadian and American warblers are migratory, with many traveling all the way to Central America and South America for the winter. A few warbler species stick around, though, and some may visit a feeding station. Warblers are characterized by their small and thin, pointed beaks.

Yellow-throated Warbler (p. 227)

- Black mask
- Yellow throat
- White patch on side of neck
- White underparts

Orange-crowned Warbler (p. 224)

- Indistinct, light eyebrow
- Short, indistinct, dusky eyeline
- Plain wing
- Yellowish-green underparts

Pine Warbler (adult male) (p. 225)

- Yellow eyering
- White belly and undertail coverts
- White wingbars
- Yellow underparts

Pine Warbler (first-year female) (p. 225)

- Whitish eyering
- Brownish upperparts
- White belly and undertail coverts
- White wingbars

Orange-crowned Warbler

Oreothlypis celata

"Western"

"Eastern"

ORANGE-CROWNED WARBLERS are very active feeders, exploring all the little nooks and crannies in bunched leaves and dried seed heads. Though they will often hover to access insects if they can't reach them from a twig, they usually stretch or hang to glean prey from leaves, flowers and the ends of branches. These acrobatic movements can help you see how the Orange-crowned Warbler got its name. The dull orange crown is not only hard to see, but it is often concealed (the species' scientific name, *celata*, means "concealed") and may even be absent in some females.

Natural Foods

Insects; spiders; occasionally nectar, sap, fruits

Feeder Fare

Suet, suet/peanut butter spread

Length: 5 inches (13 cm), similar to Black-capped Chickadee
Crown: orange on male, often concealed; may be absent on female
Eyebrow: pale, indistinct
Eyeline: short, indistinct, dusky
Eyering: indistinct, broken
Throat: dull whitish-olive in east; yellow in west
Back: olive-green
Rump: brighter olive-green
Tail: no spots
Underparts: yellowish-olive in east; yellower in west
Breast: faint streaks on sides
Undertail coverts: brighter yellow
Legs: dark
Grayer overall, especially on head, in winter

Maple Sap

We all know that maple sap is sweet, but it only has about a two to three percent sugar content (as compared to the 66 percent sugar content of maple syrup). But that is still enough to make it an energy and water source for many birds in the spring. Watch wounds in maple trees, where spring sap is dripping, and see which bird species visit.

Pine Warbler
Setophaga pinus

Spring male (*left*) and first-year female (*right*)

THIS WARBLER IS well named. Gerald Thayer wrote, "Never was a bird more aptly named than the Pine Warbler. Except when migrating, it sticks to pine woods as a cockle-bur sticks to a dog's tail" (in Chapman, 1907). These warblers are bulky looking, and their movements are almost sluggish when compared to most other warbler species.

Natural Foods

Insects; spiders; pine seeds; fruits of plants such as bayberry, sumac, Virginia creeper, grape, persimmon and dogwood; sap

Feeder Fare

Suet, suet/peanut butter spread, sunflower seeds, millet, cracked corn, peanuts, mealworms

Length: 5½ inches (14 cm), similar to Black-capped Chickadee

Eyebrow: thin, yellow

Eyering: thin, broken, yellow; whitish on first-year female

Lore: slightly dusky

Upperparts: olive-green; brown on first-year female

Wing: whitish wingbars on spring male and female; fainter wingbars on first year

Tail: white spots

Underparts: yellow; whitish, light brown wash on first year

Throat: yellow

Breast: yellow, variable dusky streaks on sides on spring male; duller, less yellow and usually no streaks on sides on spring female; only a hint of yellow on first year

Belly: white

Undertail coverts: white

Legs: dark

Duller overall in winter

First year is very brownish overall, and female is especially drab

Warbler Identification

Warblers are a tough group of birds to identify, and their sheer numbers (there are over 50 species in North America) make it even more challenging. Recognizing even the relatively few species that come to feeders can be confusing. While focusing on field marks (see page 132) is the best way for beginners to identify birds, at some point you will notice shape and size differences. Can you see the overall size, overall shape and beak shape differences between this Orange-crowned Warbler (on the left) and Pine Warbler? They are subtle, but if you can start to notice these details, you will be even better at bird identification.

Yellow-rumped Warbler

Setophaga coronata

Summer male "Myrtle"

Summer male "Audubon's"

Summer female "Myrtle"

Summer female "Audubon's"

Winter "Myrtle"

Winter "Audubon's"

FOR THIS WARBLER, it is all about the yellow. Its current name describes the bright patch above its tail. An earlier name, Yellow-crowned Warbler, points out the small yellow patch on the top of its head, which also gave it its species name, *coronata* (meaning "crowned"). These yellow patches are for showing off, as Forbush describes: "the males begin their courtship of the females, following them about and displaying their beauties by fluffing out the feathers of their sides, raising their wings and erecting the feathers of the crown, so as to exhibit to the full their beautiful black and yellow markings" (1929).

Natural Foods

Insects; spiders; fruits of plants such as bayberry, wax myrtle, viburnum, dogwood, mountain ash, juniper, poison oak and poison ivy; sap

Feeder Fare

Suet, suet/peanut butter spread, sunflower seeds, peanuts, mealworms, fruit, sugar water

Length: 5½ inches (14 cm), similar to Black-capped Chickadee
Crown: bluish-gray, yellow patch
Mask: black on "Myrtle" summer male; less black on "Audubon's" summer male
Eyebrow: broken, white on "Myrtle"
Eyering: broken, white
Throat: white on "Myrtle" summer male; yellow on "Audubon's" summer male
Breast: mottled black with streaks, yellow patch on sides; more black on "Audubon's" summer male
Back: bluish-gray with black streaks
Flanks: mottled black streaks
Wing: two white wingbars on "Myrtle" and female "Audubon's"; white patch on "Audubon's" summer male
Underparts: white
Summer female and winter are much duller and buffier overall, gray is mostly replaced by brown, and patches of yellow are smaller, especially in winter

Splitting and Lumping

Depending on current research, closely related birds are either considered to be the same species (lumping) or separate species (splitting). Yellow-rumped Warblers were once considered to be two different species: the Audubon's Warbler (in west) and the Myrtle Warbler (mostly in east). They are now lumped together in the same species. Examples of split species include the Oak Titmouse and Juniper Titmouse (which were the Plain Titmouse) and the Baltimore Oriole and Bullock's Oriole (which were the Northern Oriole).

Yellow-throated Warbler

Setophaga dominica

THIS WARBLER HAS one of the longest beaks of its family, and it puts it to good use. Unlike most warblers (except for the Black-and-white Warbler), this bird is often seen foraging on tree trunks and branches, like a nuthatch or Brown Creeper, probing its thin beak into cracks and crevices in the bark. This feeding strategy gave it its former name, Yellow-throated Creeper.

Natural Foods
Insects, spiders

Feeder Fare
Suet, suet/peanut butter spread

Length: 5½ inches (14 cm), similar to Black-capped Chickadee
Crown: black streaks, black forecrown
Eyebrow: white, may be yellow near beak
Eyeline: black
Eyering: broken, white
Cheek: black, white patch behind
Throat: yellow
Upperparts: bluish-gray
Breast: yellow upper, white lower
Belly and undertail coverts: white
Sides: black streaks
Wing: two white wingbars
Tail: white spots
Legs: dark
Females and winter males are slightly duller overall, and females have less black in crown

Fancy Meeting You Here!
Don't be surprised if on your southern vacation you come across some of your backyard birds in the palm trees. Some species, including many warblers, orioles, buntings, grosbeaks and hummingbirds, migrate to the same areas that many of us visit during the winter season. Bon voyage!

Spotted Towhee
(male) (p. 232)
- Black head and
  upperparts
- Rufous side
- White wing spots
- Underparts

Spotted Towhee
(female) (p. 232)
- Dark brown head and
  upperparts
- Rufous sides
- White wingbars
- White underparts

Eastern Towhee
(male) (p. 232)
- Black head and
  upperparts
- Rufous sides
- White underparts

Eastern Towhee
(female) (p. 232)
- Brown head and
  upperparts
- Rufous sides
- White underparts

Sparrows, Towhees and Juncos

Towhees and juncos are often the most brightly colored of our sparrows. Towhees are also much larger than our other sparrows, and they can often be found noisily scratching the ground to find food. Dark-eyed Juncos are found across North America and have many differently colored subspecies.

Canyon Towhee
(p. 233)
• Reddish cap
• Distinct upper breast streaks

California Towhee
(p. 233)
• Reddish face
• Indistinct upper breast streaks

Dark-eyed Junco
("Slate-colored") (p. 237)
• Gray head and upperparts
• Pink beak
• White belly

Dark-eyed Junco
("Oregon") (p. 237)
• Dark gray hood
• Pink beak
• Brown back
• Rufous side

Chipping Sparrow
(winter) (p. 235)
- Brown cap
- Dark eyeline
- Pinkish beak
- Plain brownish-gray breast

Chipping Sparrow
(summer) (p. 235)
- Rufous cap
- Black eyeline
- Black beak
- Plain gray breast

Field Sparrow
(p. 236)
- Rufous cap
- Rufous eyeline, behind eye only
- Pink beak
- Plain gray breast

American Tree Sparrow (p. 234)
- Rufous cap
- Rufous eyeline
- Bicolored beak
- Plain gray breast with dark central spot

Song Sparrow
(p. 239)
- Brown or rufous cap, eyeline and moustache
- Gray face and eyebrow
- White, gray or buffy breast with dark streaks and dark central spot

Fox Sparrow
("Red") (p. 238)
- Reddish cap and eyeline
- Gray eyebrow and sides of nape
- Reddish moustache
- White breast with reddish spots and reddish central spot

Fox Sparrow
("Slate-colored") (p. 238)
- Dark moustache
- Gray head
- White breast with dark spots and dark central spot
- Rufous wing

Fox Sparrow
("Sooty") (p. 238)
- Brown head
- Many brown breast spots and indistinct but large central breast spot
- White underparts

Sparrows, Towhees and Juncos

These are the confusing LBJ's (Little Brown Jobs). Most sparrows are brownish and very hard to identify for the beginner. Often found on the ground or in scrubby areas, they can be hard to see but, luckily, are often lured out into the open to feed under a bird feeder.

White-crowned Sparrow (immature) (p. 241)
- Brown and beige cap
- Brown eyeline
- Pink or orange beak
- Plain brownish-gray breast

White-crowned Sparrow (adult) (p. 241)
- Black-and-white cap
- Black eyeline
- Pinkish or yellowish beak
- Plain gray breast

White-throated Sparrow (white-striped form) (p. 240)
- Black-and-white cap
- Black eyeline
- Yellow lore spot
- Gray beak
- White throat
- Plain gray breast

White-throated Sparrow (tan-striped form) (p. 240)
- Brown and tan cap
- Dark eyeline
- Yellow lore spot
- Gray beak
- Plain brownish-gray breast (possibly with faint streaks)

Golden-crowned Sparrow (winter) (p. 242)
- Black or brownish crown with central yellowish patch
- Grayish face

Golden-crowned Sparrow (summer) (p. 242)
- Black cap with central yellow patch
- Gray face and breast

Harris's Sparrow (summer) (p. 243)
- Black crown and face
- Pink beak
- Gray head and breast

Harris's Sparrow (first winter) (p. 243)
- Dusky cap
- Pink beak
- Brown head
- Dark necklace
- White breast

Spotted Towhee and Eastern Towhee

Pipilo maculatus and *Pipilo erythrophthalmus*

Male Spotted

Male Eastern

Male Eastern "white-eyed"

Female Eastern

Female Spotted

"I HEARD A clamor in the underbrush beside me, a rustle of an animal's approach. It sounded as though the animal was about the size of a bobcat, a small bear, or a large snake. The commotion stopped and started, coming ever nearer. The agent of all this ruckus proved to be, of course, a towhee" (Annie Dillard, *Pilgrim at Tinker Creek*, 1974). What naturalist hasn't been surprised by the amount of noise a foraging towhee can make? These ground-dwelling birds are notorious for scratching loudly in leaf litter, but they can be quite difficult to see.

Natural Foods

Insects; spiders; millipedes; centipedes; snails; slugs; acorns; seeds, fruits, petals, shoots and/or buds from plants such as grasses, smartweed, blueberry, blackberry, wheat, corn and oats

Spotted

Eastern

Length: 8½ inches (21.5 cm), similar to Red-winged Blackbird
Eye: red; white in southeastern U.S.
Head and breast: black; brown on female Eastern; dark brown or grayish-brown on female Spotted
Belly: white
Side: rufous
Back: may have spots on Spotted
Upperparts: black; brown on female Eastern; dark brown or grayish-brown on female Spotted
Wing: white patches on Eastern; white wingbars or spots on Spotted
Tail: long with white corners and sides
Undertail coverts: light rufous

Feeder Fare

Sunflower seeds, millet, corn, peanuts

Eating Snow

Water is important for life, so what do non-desert-adapted birds do in cold winters, when water freezes? If there is free water available, they will be attracted to it (see page 60) and may even fly significant distances to an open water source. Sometimes you may see birds eating snow. However, melting the snow uses up some of the bird's body heat energy. There hasn't been a lot of research done on this topic, so you could look into it yourself! Do the birds eat snow on warmer-than-average days? Is it sunny or cloudy? Do only certain species do it? I've noticed that when I see birds eating snow, other nearby birds, including other species, may be doing the same thing. What do you notice?

Canyon Towhee and California Towhee

Melozone fusca and *Melozone crissalis*

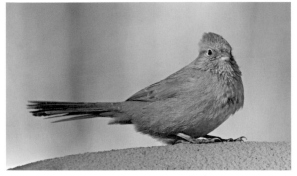

Canyon Towhee

California Towhee

Another pair of species that were once considered one species (the Brown Towhee), these two birds are actually more closely related to the large ground sparrows of Mexico and Central America than they are to Eastern or Spotted Towhees.

Natural Foods

Fruits and/or seeds of plants such as grasses, pigweed, knotweed, burr thistle, elderberry, buckthorn, poison oak, chickweed and sorrel; acorns; insects; spiders; millipedes; snails

Feeder Fare

Sunflower seeds, millet, cracked corn, peanuts

California

Canyon

Length: 9 inches (23 cm), similar to Red-winged Blackbird

Crown and eyeline: rufous

Lores and eyering: creamy on Canyon; pale rufous on California

Throat: creamy with dark spots on Canyon; pale rufous on California

Upper breast: distinct streaks or spots and possibly central spot on Canyon; indistinct on California

Upperparts and underparts: grayish-brown on Canyon; browner on California

Tail: pale tips on outer feathers on Canyon

Undertail coverts: rufous

Bathing

Watch the birds in your yard bathing. What do you notice? Do they use their wings? Do they dunk their head? Do they sit and soak first? Are certain species more nervous about being out in the open? Do some only bathe at specific times of day? There are lots of things you can notice that will connect you to your backyard birds.

American Tree Sparrow

Spizelloides arborea

WHILE THIS SPARROW breeds in the very far north of North America, it is a common winter visitor to many states and the southern parts of many provinces. It often searches the ground under feeders along with Dark-eyed Juncos.

Length: 6¼ inches (16 cm), similar to Dark-eyed Junco
Cap: rufous
Eyebrow: gray
Eyeline: rufous
Beak: bicolored
Head: gray
Breast: central spot
Back: streaked
Side: rufous wash
Wing: white wingbars
Underparts: grayish-white

Natural Foods

Grass seed; seeds of plants such as pigweed, ragweed, spruce, alder, catnip, knotweed, cinquefoil and goldenrod; insects; spiders

Feeder Fare

Sunflower seeds, millet, cracked corn, nyjer, peanuts

Open-Beak Threats

Many different birds exhibit the open-beak threat — or gaping — behavior. It is often part of an aggressive display, and birds use it to figure out if they can scare away an opponent. If one bird is clearly dominant over another, the submissive bird will likely give way. Only if the birds are well matched does an actual fight occur. Being injured is an instantly life-threatening situation for a bird, so displays help avoid as many actual physical interactions as possible.

Chipping Sparrow
Spizella passerina

Summer

Winter

Juvenile

THIS IS THE common native suburban sparrow found across most of North America. It often nests in a conifer or shrub in someone's yard, giving observers a great chance to watch its breeding cycle. It usually takes four days to make its nest. The first day all you will see is a pile of small rootlets and twigs. The second day there are more rootlets and twigs, which are arranged into a donut shape. The third day the nest has a bottom, forming a cup. The fourth day it is lined with hair. In colonial times, this bird was called the "Horsehair Bird" because it often used the tail and mane hairs of horses in its nests. Now that there are fewer horses, it may use dog or even human hair instead.

Natural Foods
Mostly grass seeds; seeds of plants such as knotweed, dandelion, bindweed, clover, chickweed, pigweed and wood sorrel; insects; spiders

Feeder Fare
Sunflower seeds, millet, cracked corn, nyjer

Length: 5½ inches (14 cm), similar to Black-capped Chickadee
Cap: reddish on summer adult; brownish on winter adult
Eyebrow: white on summer adult; buffy on winter adult
Eyeline: black on summer; dark on winter
Beak: dark on summer adult; pinkish on winter adult
Nape: gray
Throat and undertail coverts: whitish
Upperparts: streaked brown; brownish wash to flanks on winter adult
Wing: white wingbars
Rump: gray; may be brownish on first winter
Underparts: gray
First winter is a bit buffier overall

Boy or Girl?
There are usually only a few ways to tell male and female birds apart if they look the same. For Chipping Sparrows, the male does the singing and is on top during mating. The females build the nest, so they are the ones you see carrying nesting materials. Males will sometimes pick up nesting material, but they don't usually fly off with it.

Field Sparrow

Spizella pusilla

THE UNIQUE SONG of the Field Sparrow — an accelerating series of falling whistles — makes it one of the easiest bird songs to learn. Edward Samuels wrote, "Mounted on a low tree or fence-tail, he utters his pleasing, yet plaintive ditty at early morning and evening, and, in dark and cloudy weather, through the whole day" (Studer, 1881). I have heard them sing in the middle of the night as well.

Adult

Length: 5¾ inches (14.5 cm), smaller than Dark-eyed Junco
Cap: rufous
Head: gray
Eyeline: rufous, behind eye only
Eyering: white (sometimes hard to see)
Beak: pink
Upperparts: rufous or grayish with brown streaks,
Underparts: gray, usually with rufous wash on side
Rump: gray
Wing: white wingbars
Some birds are grayer overall

Juvenile

Natural Foods

Mostly grass seeds; insects

Feeder Fare

Sunflower seeds, cracked corn, millet

Sparrows with Rufous Caps

Chipping Sparrow
Eyeline: black
Eyebrow: white
Beak: black

American Tree Sparrow
Eyeline: rufous
Eyebrow: gray
Beak: bicolored

Field Sparrow
Eyeline: rufous with white eyering
Eyebrow: gray
Beak: pink

**Immature
White-crowned Sparrow**
Eyeline: dull rufous
Eyebrow: buffy
Beak: pink or orange

Dark-eyed Junco
Junco hyemalis

"Slate-colored"

"Red-backed"

"Gray-headed"

"Oregon"

"White-winged"

"Pink-sided"

JUNCOS ARE OFTEN ranked the most common feeder bird in North America. Though they vary greatly across the continent, their white outer tail feathers are always there to help you identify them. This species is made up of many different subspecies. Identifiable "groups" include the following: "Slate-colored," "White-winged," "Oregon," "Pink-sided," "Red-backed" and "Gray-headed."

Natural Foods
Seeds from plants such as grasses, timothy, ragweed, pigweed, knotweed and lamb's-quarters; insects; spiders

Feeder Fare
Sunflower seeds, millet, safflower seeds, nyjer, cracked corn, peanuts

Weird Hybrid
As if juncos weren't already complicated enough, there have been records of them hybridizing with White-throated Sparrows! These two birds are not even in the same genus and have completely different songs. Genetic research has shown that *Junco* and *Zonotrichia* sparrows separated into different species 1.3 to 6.6 million years ago, but it seems the birds don't always know that.

Length: 6¼ inches (16 cm)
"SLATE-COLORED"
Head, upperparts and breast: slate gray
Beak: pink
Belly and undertail coverts: white
Tail: white outer feathers
First-year male and adult female are paler overall, with variable brownish wash and lighter gray edges on wings
First-winter female also has more brownish wash, especially on sides.
Other groups are similar to "Slate-colored," except as noted below (at group boundaries, some of these characteristics may blend together, so it can be hard to tell these birds apart):
"WHITE-WINGED"
Body: paler gray overall
Wing: white wingbars
"OREGON"
Hood: dark gray
Body: brown
Side: brown or rufous
"PINK-SIDED"
Hood: gray
Lores: dark
Throat: pale gray
Side: rufous
"RED-BACKED"
Lores: dark
Beak: bicolored
Back: reddish-brown patch
"GRAY-HEADED"
Lores: dark
Beak: pink
Back: reddish-brown patch

Fox Sparrow
Passerella iliaca

"Red"

"Sooty"

"Slate-colored"

"Thick-billed"

A SINGLE FOX Sparrow stayed at my childhood bird feeders for a few consecutive winters. I loved to think that it was always the same one, and since many bird species do winter in the same spot each year, maybe it was. I enjoyed watching how its backward kick-scratching sent the leaves or snow flying as it looked for fallen seeds under the feeder. This species is made up of many subspecies that are organized into four groups: "Red," "Sooty," "Slate-colored" and "Thick-billed."

Natural Foods
Seeds and/or fruits of plants such as of blueberry, raspberry, elderberry, pokeweed, rose, grape, serviceberry, grass, sedge, ragweed and sorrel

Feeder Fare
Sunflower seeds, millet, nyjer, cracked corn, safflower seeds

Speciation
Speciation is the process by which one species evolves into more than one species. There are many ways this can happen, but the most common one seems to be when two populations of the same species become isolated from each other. Fox Sparrows appear to be in the process of becoming four species, with each subspecies adapting to a particular location.

Length: 7 inches (18 cm), similar to Downy Woodpecker

"RED"

Cap and face: rufous

Head: gray

Breast: white with rufous streaks and often a large breast spot

Belly: white

Side: rufous streaks

Upperparts: rufous streaks

Wing: thin white wingbars

Rump: gray

"SOOTY"

Upperparts: dark brown with very large breast spot

Underparts: white and heavily spotted

Undertail coverts: dark

"SLATE-COLORED" AND "THICK-BILLED"

Head, back and rump: gray

Beak: very large on "Thick-billed"

Wing and tail: rufous with thin wingbars on "Slate-colored"; fainter or no wingbars on "Thick-billed"

Breast: central spot

Underparts: white with dark spots/streaks

Song Sparrow
Melospiza melodia

"Eastern"

"Western"

MARGARET MORSE NICE, one of ornithology's best pioneering researchers, wrote in 1937 of the Song Sparrow: "There is a large population right at my door; no time is wasted going to and from the field of study and I am able to keep track of my subjects all the time . . . the song sparrow is an abundant, widely distributed, friendly and attractive bird" (in Bent, 1968). If you get to know this common species well, you will be able to identify other, less commonly seen, sparrows by comparison. It will also give you a chance to learn about its breeding biology and different behaviors.

Length: 6¼ inches (16 cm), similar to Dark-eyed Junco
Breast: white with thick brown streaks, usually with a strong central spot
Upperparts: brown with streaks
Wing: very thin white wingbars
Tail: long, rounded; pumps tail in flight
Different populations of Song Sparrows may be darker or more rufous than others

Natural Foods
Seeds and/or fruits of plants such as grass, pigweed, knotweed, clover, dock, smartweed, sheep sorrel, mulberry, blackberry, cherry, strawberry and blueberry; insects; spiders; earthworms

Feeder Fare
Sunflower seeds, millet, cracked corn, peanut, nyjer

Margaret's Sparrow
Margaret Morse Nice studied many bird species, but she made her biggest mark through her studies of the Song Sparrows that lived in her Ohio neighborhood in the 1920s and 1930s. She studied everything about the lives of these common sparrows, including territoriality, longevity, pairing, nesting and feeding — all while raising her five children. She even modified plastic from children's toys to make colored leg bands (see page 171) to identify each individual sparrow. Her Song Sparrow study was revolutionary in its understanding of bird biology, and many of her findings are still referred to today, in current studies of our birds.

White-throated Sparrow

Zonotrichia albicollis

White-striped

Tan-striped

First year

USING MADE-UP phrases for bird songs is a great way to learn them. It is fun to make up your own, but learning established ones is also enjoyable. Sometimes there are regional differences to these phrases. For example, in the United States, the White-throated Sparrow is said to sing "Old Sam Peabody, Peabody, Peabody, Peabody." But north of the border, the song is known as "Home Sweet Canada, Canada, Canada, Canada."

Natural Foods

Seeds, fruits, buds and/or blossoms of plants such as grasses, blueberry, raspberry, grape, rose, viburnum, maple, sumac, mountain ash and elm; insects; spiders; snails; centipedes; millipedes

Feeder Fare

Millet, sunflower, cracked corn

Length: 6¾ inches (17 cm), similar to Downy Woodpecker
Crown: black with white central stripe on white-striped; dark brown with tan central stripe on tan-striped
Eyebrow: white on white-striped; tan on tan-striped
Lores: yellow on white-striped; duller yellow on tan-striped
Eyeline: dark
Cheek: gray
Face and underparts: buffy wash on tan-striped
Throat: white
Breast: gray; sometimes faint streaks on tan-striped
Back: brown streaks
Rump: brownish
Wing: white wingbars
First winter is similar to adult tan-striped but has darker breast streaking and sometimes has a central breast spot

Special Mating System

The two color morphs, white-striped and tan-striped, occur equally within males and females. Interestingly, each pair is usually made up of one of each morph. In general, white-striped birds are more aggressive (good for keeping a territory) and less parental (bad for raising young) than tan-striped birds. And so, white-striped females choose the good-parenting tan-striped males, leaving the tan-striped females with the white-striped males. This is the only bird species in the world that has this kind of mating system.

White-crowned Sparrow
Zonotrichia leucophrys

Adult

Immature

I LIKE TO call this sparrow the "skunk-headed sparrow" — for obvious reasons. This species is one of the most studied songbirds in the world: scientists have studied details about its physiology, geographical variation, breeding biology, migration patterns and song development. But for backyard bird-watchers, it is just nice to have a sparrow that is easy to identify!

Length: 7 inches (18 cm), similar to Downy Woodpecker
Crown: black with white central stripe on adult; brown with buffy central stripe on first winter
Eyebrow: white on adult; buffy on first winter
Eyeline: black on adult; brown on first winter
Beak: pink or orange
Cheek and neck: gray on adult; buffy cheek on first winter
Underparts: gray
Back: brownish streaks
Rump: grayish-brown
Flanks: brown
Wing: white wingbars

Natural Foods
Seeds and/or fruit of plants such as grasses, smartweed, chickweed, oats, dock, pigweed, ragweed, sunflower, goosefoot, elderberry and blackberry; insects

Feeder Fare
Sunflower seeds, millet, cracked corn

Not Working . . .
Fake owls are often used to keep birds (usually pigeons and gulls) away from certain areas. These may work, but it seems this one has lost its effectiveness, at least for this particular White-crowned Sparrow! Another fun photo.

Golden-crowned Sparrow
Zonotrichia atricapilla

Summer adult

Winter adult

First winter

UNLIKE ITS CLOSE relative the White-crowned Sparrow, the Golden-crowned Sparrow's breeding biology has not been studied extensively. It breeds in remote parts of the Northwest, but, luckily for West Coast feeder watchers, it is a common winter bird from southern British Columbia to southern California.

Natural Foods
Seeds, buds, flowers and/or fruits of plants such as grasses, pigweed, dock, nightshade, starwort, knotweed, chickweed, turkey mullein, apple, elderberry, oats, poison oak, wheat and tarweed; insects; spiders

Feeder Fare
Millet, sunflower seeds, cracked corn, safflower seeds, peanuts

Length: 7¼ inches (18.5 cm), similar to Brown-headed Cowbird
Cap: black with yellow and white center in summer; less black on head in winter; no black on first winter
Forehead and lore: some yellow on first winter
Eyeline: indistinct on winter
Head: gray
Beak: dark upper and pale lower mandibles in summer; more uniform gray in winter
Back: brown with dark streaks
Wing: white wingbars
Rump: brown
Underparts: gray
Flanks: brown
Undertail coverts: white

All That Glitters Is Not Gold . . .
If you were a gold miner, you may well think that seeing this sparrow — with its golden cap — near your mining site is a good sign. Not so. Miners of the late 1800s and early 1900s thought this bird was singing "no gold here!"

Harris's Sparrow

Zonotrichia querula

Summer adult

Winter adult

First winter

THE HARRIS'S SPARROW is the only bird in the world that only nests within Canada's borders. Its extremely remote breeding range made its nest one of the last North American bird nests to be found. From the time the bird was first described by Europeans, it took almost a century for them to discover the first nest.

Natural Foods

Seeds and/or fruits of plants such as grasses, sedge, ragweed, goosefoot, knotweed, bearberry, crowberry and cranberry; young spruce needles; insects; spiders

Feeder Fare

Millet, sunflower seeds, cracked corn

Length: 7½ inches (19 cm), similar to Brown-headed Cowbird

Head: gray in summer; brown in winter

Crown: black on adult; dark and less extensive on first winter

Face: black on adult; brown on first winter

Throat: black on adult; white often bordered with black on first winter

Beak: pink

Upper breast: black on adults; some streaks on first winter

Underparts: white

Side: dark streaks

Back: brown with dark streaks

Rump: grayish-brown

Wing: thin white wingbars

Badge of Dominance

Harris's Sparrows have variable dark throats. Older males have more black in their throats, and this shows other birds in their flock that they are experienced and dominant individuals. This reduces fighting since young and older males can visually tell each other apart, without having to physically assess each other. It is thought that the spot patterns on the breast also distinguish individuals, so birds with similar bib sizes can recognize each other after they have fought, thus reducing the number of fights in the future.

Summer Tanager
(first-summer male)
(p. 246)
• Yellowish with red
  patches overall
• Large beak

Summer Tanager
(male) (p. 246)
• Bright red overall
• Large beak

Scarlet Tanager
(male) (p. 246)
• Bright scarlet-red overall
• Black wing

Western Tanager
(male) (p. 247)
• Orangey-red head
• Black upperparts
• Yellow and white
  wingbars
• Yellow underparts

Tremendous Tanagers and Captivating Cardinals

Tanagers and cardinals are in different families, but they do share an important color feature: red. The red on male tanagers seems to glow. These birds are migrants in most of North America. Northern Cardinals and Pyrrhuloxias, however, are year-round residents in their ranges. Their distinctive crests and seed-eating diets rank them high on feeder providers' most-wanted lists.

Western Tanager
(winter male) (p. 247)
- Some orangey-red on face
- Dark upperparts
- Yellow and white wingbars
- Yellow underparts

Western Tanager
(female) (p. 247)
- Grayish-olive overall
- Grayish back
- Wingbars

Scarlet Tanager
(female) (p. 246)
- Yellowish overall
- Dusky wing

Summer Tanager
(female) (p. 246)
- Yellowish overall
- Large beak

Pyrrhuloxia
(male) (p. 249)
- Gray overall
- Red highlights on crest, face, wing, tail and center of breast
- Stubby yellow beak

Pyrrhuloxia
(female) (p. 249)
- Grayish-beige overall
- Red highlights on crest, wing and tail
- Faint mask
- Stubby yellowish beak

Northern Cardinal
(male) (p. 248)
- All red
- Crest
- Black mask
- Red-orange beak

Northern Cardinal
(female) (p. 248)
- Brownish overall
- Red highlights on crest, wing and tail
- Black mask
- Red-orange beak

Summer Tanager and Scarlet Tanager

Piranga rubra and *Piranga olivacea*

Adult male (*left*), first-summer male (*center*) and adult female (*right*) Summer Tanager

Adult male (*left*), orange-variant male (*center*) and adult female (*right*) Scarlet Tanager

TANAGERS ARE VERY common in Central and South America, where there are many species and a rainbow of colors and patterns. North of the Mexican border, there are only four regularly occurring tanager species, and all have red as their brightest color — and what a red it is!

Natural Foods

Insects; spiders; snails; earthworms; fruits of plants such as blackberry, blueberry, huckleberry, serviceberry, strawberry, chokeberry, mulberry and pokeweed

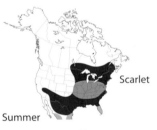

Scarlet

Summer

■ both

Feeder Fare

Suet/peanut butter spread, fruits, jellies, mealworms, sugar water, possibly some seeds

SUMMER TANAGER

Length: 7¾ inches (19.5 cm), similar to Brown-headed Cowbird

Male is bright red overall

Beak: pale or gray

Female and first-summer male are yellowish-olive overall; older females have some orange; first-summer male often has variably red head and body with red patches

SCARLET TANAGER

Length: 7 inches (18 cm), shorter than Brown-headed Cowbird

Male

Bright crimson-red, or sometimes orange, overall; in fall and winter, red is replaced with yellowish-green

Wing and tail: black

Beak: gray

Female

Upperparts: yellowish-olive

Wing and tail: dusky, rarely with faint wingbars

Underparts: yellow

Berry Nice!

Many birds that primarily eat insects, such as tanagers, vireos and some warblers, start adding fruits to their diets just before fall migration begins. Their digestive tracts take a few days to adjust, but then the birds start laying down the fat that they need for long, southern flights. Birds that find a berry bush or wild grape vine can eat more and eat faster than when they search for insects. The fruit also provides much needed micronutrients that help with the stresses of migration. And the plants benefit because the birds disperse their seeds. Win-win!

Western Tanager

Piranga ludoviciana

Summer male

Winter male

Adult female

THIS TANAGER BREEDS farther north than any other of the more than 200 members of its family, making it all the way to Canada's Northwest Territories. They may only spend two months on their northern breeding grounds before they start migrating south again.

Length: 7¼ inches (18.5 cm), similar to Brown-headed Cowbird

Head: red on summer male; red only around face on winter male; no red on female

Back and tail: black on male; grayish on female

Wing: black on male; grayish on female; both sexes have yellow and white wingbars

Nape, rump and underparts: yellow

Winter male is duller overall

Female is more grayish-olive overall

Natural Foods
Insects; fruits of plants such as elderberry, cherry, hawthorn, serviceberry, mulberry, blackberry, juniper and grape

Feeder Fare
Suet/peanut butter spread, fruits, jellies, mealworms, sunflower seeds, sugar water

Special Red Heads
Unlike the reds of Scarlet and Summer Tanagers, the Western Tanager's red comes from a relatively uncommon pigment called rhodoxanthin. This pigment has only been found in a few, mostly tropical, bird species. Recently, it has been showing up in some aberrantly feathered eastern North American birds, such as Cedar Waxwings that have an orange-tipped tail instead of the regular yellow-tipped tail. It is thought that the berries of introduced honeysuckles are the source of these odd feather colors. In contrast, it appears that Western Tanagers get this rare pigment from insects that they eat (and these insects get the pigment from the plants they eat).

Northern Cardinal

Cardinalis cardinalis

Adult male

Adult female

PROBABLY THE FAVORITE feeder bird in the East, the Northern Cardinal is one of those birds that you just can't believe lives in your backyard. Its range has been expanding northward for the past 200 years, so even more people can marvel at its lovely crest and brilliant feathers. Northern Cardinals can visit feeders at any time of day, but they are most likely to arrive near dawn or dusk.

Natural Foods

Fruits and/or seeds of plants such as grape, dogwood, hackberry, mulberry, sumac, tulip tree, smartweed, vervain, corn, oats, blackberry, sedge, grasses, doveweed and knotweed; insects; spiders; centipedes; snails; slugs

Feeder Fare

Sunflower seeds, safflower seeds, cracked corn, millet, peanuts

Length: 8¾ inches (22 cm), similar to Red-winged Blackbird

ADULT MALE

All red

Crest: large

Face: black

Beak: red or orange

Back: grayish-red

Tail long, rounded

ADULT FEMALE

Body: warm brown

Crest, wing and tail: reddish

Face: blackish

Beak: orange

Tail: long, rounded

See Sally Sing!

In Canada and the United States, it is mostly male birds that sing. They use singing to proclaim their territorial rights as well as to attract a mate. In the tropics, however, many bird species also have female singers. Scientists theorize that nonmigratory tropical females may sing to help defend their yearlong territories. When we do find a singing female in our area, she may also be using song as an aggressive behavior related to territory. The female Northern Cardinal pictured here was alternately singing and attacking her reflection in one of my windows; she was clearly trying to intimidate the "intruder."

Pyrrhuloxia
Cardinalis sinuatus

Adult male

LIKE NORTHERN CARDINALS, Pyrrhuloxias are very territorial during the breeding season. However, in areas where winters are cold, they often form large flocks that look for food en masse. Some of these flocks can have up to 1000 birds!

Length: 8¾ inches (22 cm), similar to Red-winged Blackbird
Male is gray overall; female is browner overall
Face, crest, throat, wing edge, belly and outer tail feathers: red on male; less red on female
Beak: yellow, stubby; duller on female

Adult female

Natural Foods
Seeds and/or fruits of plants such as grasses, doveweed, pigweed, cactus and nightshade

Feeder Fare
Sunflower seeds, cracked corn, peanuts

That's My Cousin!
Not all birds that look the same are related (see Black-headed Grosbeak, page 253), but the Pyrrhuloxia and the Northern Cardinal are close relatives. They are in the same genus, *Cardinalis*. Even though these two species have overlapping ranges and seem very similar to us, hybridization has only been recorded once.

Painted Bunting
(male) (p. 255)
• Bright blue head
• Red eyering
• Red throat and
  underparts
• Green back and wings

Lazuli Bunting
(male) (p. 255)
• Bright blue head and
  upperparts
• Orange breast
• White wingbars
• White underparts

Indigo Bunting
(male) (p. 254)
• All bright blue

Blue Grosbeak
(male) (p. 254)
• Bright blue overall
• Large beak
• Black mask
• Chestnut wingbars

Gorgeous Grosbeaks and Beautiful Buntings

These songsters surely have the best and brightest color combinations at our feeders, or at least the males do. The females are drab but still lovely, with either patterned or plain plumage. All have seed-eating beak shapes.

Rose-breasted Grosbeak (male) (p. 252)
- Black head
- Large pink beak
- Red breast triangle
- Black upperparts
- White wing patches
- White underparts

Black-headed Grosbeak (male) (p. 253)
- Black head
- Large gray beak
- Orange collar and underparts
- Black upperparts
- White wing patches

Black-headed Grosbeak (female) (p. 253)
- Broad white eyebrow
- Large beak
- Thin streaks on whitish to orangey breast
- White wingbars

Rose-breasted Grosbeak (female) (p. 252)
- Broad white eyebrow
- Large beak
- Dark streaks on whitish breast
- White wingbars

Painted Bunting (female) (p. 255)
- Greenish upperparts
- Buffy to yellowish underparts

Lazuli Bunting (female) (p. 255)
- Brown upperparts
- Thin, pale wingbars
- Lighter underparts

Indigo Bunting (female) (p. 254)
- Fine, faint streaks on breast
- Brown upperparts
- Lighter underparts

Blue Grosbeak (female) (p. 254)
- All brown
- Large beak
- Chestnut wingbars
- May have some blue highlights in wing

Rose-breasted Grosbeak

Pheucticus ludovicianus

Adult male

Adult female

First-year male

NOT MANY BIRDS grab the viewer's attention like the male Rose-breasted Grosbeak. Its brilliant red chest shield beams from its body's black-and-white patterns. But this species is a feast for your ears as well as your eyes. Jacob Studer wrote, "The Rose-breasted Grosbeak is, in common opinion, one of the sweetest singers of this continent . . . his notes are clear, full, and very loud, suddenly changing, at times, to a plaintive and melancholy, but exceedingly sweet, cadence" (1881).

Natural Foods

Insects; fruits, seeds, buds and/or flowers of plants such as elderberry, blackberry, raspberry, serviceberry, mulberry, grasses, pigweed, smartweed and sunflower

Feeder Fare

Sunflower seeds, cracked corn, safflower seeds, fruits

Length: 8 inches (20.5 cm), similar to Brown-headed Cowbird
MALE
Head: black
Beak: pink
Breast: red triangle
Back: black
Rump: white
Wing: white patches
Underparts: white
First-year males have brownish flight feathers and less black and red overall
Some first-year males are similar to females but may have a rich orangish-buff breast or small reddish patches
FEMALE
Crown: brown with light central stripe
Eyebrow: white
Breast and side: streaks
Upperparts: brownish streaks
Wing: white wingbars
Underparts: white
Winter females may have a buffy wash on breast

Gender Dominance

Here, a male Rose-breasted Grosbeak shows a female who's boss. These aggressive interactions may even happen during the start of pair formation. Males may chase a female, but less intensely than when they chase other males. Eventually the tables may turn, and the female may chase the male after he does some of his courtship displays.

Black-headed Grosbeak

Pheucticus melanocephalus

Adult male

Adult female

First-year male

SOME FIRST-YEAR male Black-headed Grosbeaks can look female-like, and some are closer to an adult male's plumage. The ones that look like females avoid being attacked by adult males, while the ones that look like adult males are more likely to be attacked. So why don't they all just look like females? Because the ones that look like adult males have a chance to defend a territory and breed, whereas the female-like males have to wait another year to nest.

Natural Foods

Insects; spiders; snails; fruits and/or seeds of plants such as wheat, oats, mulberry, strawberry, crab apple, cherry, blackberry, serviceberry, poison oak, elderberry, nightshade, dock, chickweed, milk thistle, pigweed, geranium, smartweed, mallow, elm and sumac

Feeder Fare

Sunflower seeds, cracked corn, jellies, sugar water

The Nose Knows . . . Or Does It?

Not everyone with a big nose is related, right? The same can be said for grosbeaks. Having a large beak (*gros* means "large" in French) is an adaptation that allows these birds to crack open hard seeds. But not all birds with a big beak are closely related. Evening and Pine Grosbeaks are in a different family than the other three grosbeaks, and thus they are not very closely related to them. And while Black-headed and Rose-breasted Grosbeaks are very closely related (they're in same genus, called *Pheuticus*) and can even interbreed, their other family member, the Blue Grosbeak, is actually more closely related to Lazuli, Indigo, Painted and Varied Buntings (which are all in the genus *Passerina*).

Length: 8¼ inches (21 cm), similar to Brown-headed Cowbird

MALE

Head: black on adult; brown on first year

Eyebrow: orange or white on first year

Moustache: white on first year

Beak: large, gray

Nape, rump and underparts: rusty-orange

Belly: yellowish

Back: dark streaks

Wings: black with white patches on adult; brown with white patches on first year

Tail: black on adult; brown on first year

Some first-year males are very female-like

FEMALE

Streaky brown overall

Eyebrow: white

Breast: fine streaks on side

Wing: white wingbars

Underparts: whitish with orangey wash on sides and flanks (more orange in winter)

Blue Grosbeak and Indigo Bunting

Passerina caerulea and *Passerina cyanea*

Blue Grosbeak: adult male (*left*), adult female (*center*), first-summer male (*right*)

Indigo Bunting: adult male (*left*), adult female (*center*), first-summer male (*right*)

THE MALE PLUMAGE of these two species just screams BLUE! Both the Blue Grosbeak and the Indigo Bunting like scrubby areas and forest edges, where they belt out their songs for all to hear.

Natural Foods

Insects; spiders; snails; seeds, buds, flowers and/or fruits of plants such as grasses, wheat, oats, corn, rice, alfalfa, dandelion, vetch, goldenrod, thistle, serviceberry, blueberry, blackberry, dogwood, strawberry, elderberry, elm, aspen, oak, beech, walnut, hickory and maple

Feeder Fare

Millet, sunflower seeds, nyjer, cracked corn

Length:

Blue Grosbeak: 6¾ inches (17 cm), similar to Brown-headed Cowbird

Indigo Bunting: 5½ inches (14 cm), similar to Black-capped Chickadee

MALE

Bright blue overall

Beak: gray; larger on Blue Grosbeak

Wing: chestnut wingbars on Blue Grosbeak

First-summer male is similar to adult female but has variable blue patches overall.

First-winter male Blue Grosbeak is richer brown overall.

FEMALE

Brown overall; richer brown on first-winter Blue Grosbeak

Throat: lighter

Wing and tail: faint blue highlights; light chestnut wingbars on Blue Grosbeak

Breast: faint, blurry streaks on Indigo Bunting

Belly and undertail coverts: whitish on Indigo Bunting

Blue Grosbeak

Indigo Bunting

Understanding Migration

In the 1960s, researchers used Indigo Buntings to help us understand bird migration. They put buntings into funnels placed with the wide end at the top, which was left open so the birds could see out. At the narrow end, they put ink pads. The birds were left standing on the ink pads, and then they were shown the stars in a planetarium, which would prompt them to fly (since most small birds migrate at night). By studying the amount of ink that the birds left on the sides of the funnel, as they tried to fly in a particular direction, the researchers could see that the birds were using the stars to navigate!

Lazuli Bunting and Painted Bunting

Passerina amoena and *Passerina ciris*

Lazuli: summer male (*left*), winter male (*center*), female (*right*)   Painted: male (*right*), first-year female (*right*)

LAZULI BUNTING (and possibly Painted Bunting) males learn their songs in their first spring, when they are almost a year old. They listen to other adult males singing and pick phrases out of those songs to make up one of their own.

Natural Foods

Insects; spiders; snails; seeds and/or fruits of plants such as grasses, sedge, chickweed, filaree, serviceberry, chokecherry, wood sorrel, spurge, pigweed, dock, pine, rose, wheat and fig

Lazuli

Painted

Feeder Fare

Millet, sunflower seed, nyjer

Length: 5½ inches (14 cm), similar to Black-capped Chickadee

LAZULI BUNTING

Male

Breast: orange

Belly and undertail coverts: white

Upperparts: bright blue

Wing: white wingbars

Brown wash overall in winter

Female

Grayish-brown overall

Underparts: lighter

Wing: thin and pale wingbars

Tail: some blue highlights

Underparts: oranger, less blue highlights in winter

PAINTED BUNTING

Head: blue on male

Eyering: red on male

Back: green

Upperparts: green on first-year male and female

Underparts: red on adult male; yellowish on first-year male and female

First-year female duller overall

Lazuli Lessons

Lazuli is a reference to the bright blue color of the lapis lazuli stone. Many other birds have names that describe different variations of blue, such as indigo, azure, cobalt, cerulean, sapphire and ultramarine. But, unlike yellows and reds, blue pigments do not occur in feathers. Instead, the blue coloration comes from the feather's structure, which reflects blue light to our eyes. This is why the brilliant blues of jays, bluebirds and buntings can be hard to see in low light.

Red-winged Blackbird (male) (p. 260)
- Black overall
- Dark eye
- Red shoulder

Red-winged Blackbird (young winter male) (p. 260)
- Black overall
- Rusty feather edges
- Dark eye
- Red shoulder

Rusty Blackbird (male) (p. 261)
- Slightly iridescent overall
- Yellow eye
- Thin beak
- Purplish iridescence on head
- Green iridescence on body

Brewer's Blackbird (male) (p. 261)
- Very iridescent overall
- Yellow eye
- Very pointed, conical beak
- Purplish head and green body

Red-winged Blackbird (female) (p. 260)
- Buffy eyebrow
- Dark eyeline
- Streaked body

Rusty Blackbird (winter male) (p. 261)
- Rusty feather edges
- Light eyebrow
- Yellow eye
- Dark eyeline and mask

Rusty Blackbird (winter female) (p. 261)
- Light brown overall
- Light eyebrow
- Yellow eye
- Dark eyeline and mask

Brewer's Blackbird (female) (p. 261)
- Brown overall
- Dark eye
- Pointed beak

Bold Blackbirds

Many of our male blackbirds have a colorful shine to their feathers, making them some of our most gorgeous feeder visitors. However, some of these species are very hard to tell apart. Usually, though, at least one of the genders has a good ID feature. If they show up in pairs, be sure to look at both carefully. The range maps can also help you decide which species are common in your area.

Common Grackle
(adult) (p. 262)
- Iridescent purple, blue, green and/or bronze overall
- Yellow eye
- Long tail

Boat-tailed Grackle
(male) (p. 263)
- Iridescent purple, blue and/or green overall
- Brown or yellow eye
- Very long tail

Great-tailed Grackle
(male) (p. 263)
- Iridescent purple, blue and/or green overall
- Yellow eye
- Very long beak
- Very long tail

Brown-headed Cowbird
(male) (p. 259)
- Brown head
- Short beak
- Glossy black body

Common Grackle
(juvenile) (p. 262)
- Brown overall
- Dark eye

Boat-tailed Grackle
(female) (p. 263)
- Brown or yellow eye
- Light brown underparts

Great-tailed Grackle
(female) (p. 263)
- Darker brown overall
- Light eyebrow
- Yellow eye

Brown-headed Cowbird (female)
(p. 259)
- Brown overall
- Dark eye
- Short beak

Eastern Meadowlark and Western Meadowlark

Sturnella magna and *Sturnella neglecta*

THESE TWO BIRDS look the same but have been considered separate species for over 100 years. Voice is the best way to tell them apart: The Western has a rich, bubbly series of clear whistles that fall in pitch and jumble at the end. The Eastern sings higher, thinner notes with no jumble and sounds a bit like "sweet spring is here."

Length: 9½ inches (24 cm), shorter than Red-winged Blackbird
Beak: long, pointed
Eyebrow: yellow and white
Breast: black "V"
Upperparts: mottled brown
Tail: short
Underparts: bright yellow

Eastern Meadowlark

Natural Foods
Insects; seeds and/or fruits of plants such as grasses, corn, sunflower, oats, wheat, bayberry and pine

Feeder Fare
Sunflower seeds, cracked corn

Western Meadowlark

The Six-State Songster

The gorgeous, clear song of the Western Meadowlark has helped make it the official state bird of Kansas, Montana, Nebraska, North Dakota, Oregon and Wyoming. However, the top choice for state bird is the Northern Cardinal, which holds seven titles. The Northern Mockingbird used to be tied with the Western Meadowlark for second place, but in 1948 the state of South Carolina changed its state bird from the mockingbird to the Carolina Wren.

Brown-headed Cowbird

Molothrus ater

Adult male

Adult female

Juvenile

THIS IS ONE of the least favorite backyard birds, due to its habit of laying its eggs in other birds' nests (see below) — but don't think it's lazy. If a small songbird pair is able to raise two nests of young in a season, the female will lay around 8 to 10 eggs in total. But the female Brown-headed Cowbird may lay 40 eggs in one season! So it might look easy, but it still takes a lot of energy.

Natural Foods

Seeds of plants such as grasses, ragweed, oats, corn, knotweed and doveweed; insects

Feeder Fare

Sunflower seeds, millet, cracked corn, peanuts

Length: 7½ inches (19 cm)
Male is black overall; female and juvenile are very drab brown overall (females can be hard to identify)
Beak: short (for a blackbird)
Head: shiny brown on male
Breast: some streaking on juvenile

Nest Parasitism

Brown-headed Cowbirds never make their own nest. The female always lays her eggs in the nest of other birds. Over 220 species of birds have had Brown-headed Cowbird eggs laid in their nests, and while many of those eggs will be rejected by their host, 144 species have successfully raised cowbird chicks to fledging. The size of these successful host birds ranges from tiny kinglets to heavy meadowlarks. The Chipping Sparrow, shown here feeding a cowbird chick, is the fourth most common Brown-headed Cowbird host species, after the Yellow Warbler, Song Sparrow and Red-eyed Vireo.

Red-winged Blackbird

Agelaius phoeniceus

Adult male

Adult female

Young male

ONE OF THE first birds that beginning birders can identify, the Red-winged Blackbird is well named and easy to distinguish, with the male's black coloring and distinctive red wing patch. The male is a busy guy: he may have up to 15 females nesting in his territory, whereas most birds only have one mate. He has to work hard to keep these females to himself, though; genetic work shows that some of the young in his nests are actually sired by a different male.

Natural Foods

Insects; seeds of plants such as corn, wheat, ragweed, cocklebur, sunflower, sorghum and rice

Feeder Fare

Sunflower seeds, millet, cracked corn, peanuts

Length: 8¾ inches (22 cm)
MALE
All black
Beak: pointed
Shoulder: red patch, usually bordered by yellow
First-summer male ranges in appearance from female-like to male-like
FEMALE
Eyebrow: buffy
Throat and shoulder: may show orange on older females
Upperparts: brown
Underparts: buffy, heavily streaked with brown

The Weight of the World Is on His Shoulders

For male Red-winged Blackbirds, the weight of their world is actually on their shoulders. This male is doing his "song spread" display, which shows off his epaulettes to their fullest. This display helps him defend his territory from rivals. Males that are trying to intrude on a strong male's territory may cover their red epaulettes with black feathers, so they are less likely to get attacked; you may see this at your feeder in the spring.

Brewer's Blackbird and Rusty Blackbird

Euphagus cyanocephalus and *Euphagus carolinus*

Brewer's: summer male (*left*), female (*right*)   Rusty: summer male (*left*), winter male (*center*), winter female (*right*)

THE RUSTY BLACKBIRD breeds farther north than any other blackbird species. And it has another claim to fame: it is likely the only blackbird who has had its old nest used by a sandpiper. (Although sandpipers primarily live and nest on the ground, Solitary Sandpipers have been known to use the Rusty Blackbird's bulky tree nest.) The Rusty's preference for a breeding habitat of northern bogs, fens, muskegs or swamps contrasts with that of the Brewer's Blackbird, which nests in a variety of habitats, such as fields, suburbs, meadows, pastures, golf courses, river edges and farmland.

Natural Foods
Insects; spiders; acorns; seeds and/or fruits of plant such as pine, grasses, grape, beech, corn, oats, wheat, holly, dogwood and black gum; Rusty also eats crayfish, small fish, salamanders

Feeder Fare
Sunflower seeds, millet, cracked corn

Length: 9 inches (23 cm), similar to Red-winged Blackbird

RUSTY BLACKBIRD
Summer male is black overall with faint purple and green gloss; summer female is grayish-brown overall; winter male is black overall with rusty edges; winter female is more buffy overall
Eyebrow: rusty on winter male
Eye: yellow
Lores: dusky on female
Beak: thin, slightly curved

BREWER'S BLACKBIRD
Summer male is black overall with purple and green gloss; winter male has brownish edges overall, especially on head; female is brown overall
Eyes: yellow on male; dark (rarely yellow) on female
Beak: straight, pointed and conical

Remembering Songs

Reading phrases to learn bird songs is hard enough, but you also have to remember them. Try to make associations with the phrase and the bird. For example, Rusty Blackbirds have a song that sounds like a squeaky gate — the gate is rusty. A Field Sparrow's whistle is like the pattern of a soccer ball's accelerating bounce in a field. Eastern Meadowlarks sing "sweet spring is here," and they are one of the first migrants to many areas in the spring. What associations can you make to help you remember?

Brewer's
Blackbird

Rusty
Blackbird

Common Grackle

Quiscalus quiscula

THE IRIDESCENCE OF the Common Grackle's plumage is mesmerizing. A six-year-old junior naturalist in one of my classes called them "those oil birds" because the glossy colors reminded him of a drop of oil on wet pavement. Even John James Audubon was impressed. In 1831, he wrote, "The genial rays of the sun shine on their silky plumage offers . . . rich and varying tints, that no painter, however gifted, could ever imitate them" (1999).

Adult

Length: 12½ inches (32 cm), longer than Blue or Steller's Jay
Adult is completely black; juvenile is brown overall
Eye: yellow on adult; brown on juvenile
Beak: long, pointed
Head: iridescent blue
Body: highlights of bronze, green and/or purple
Tail: long, may be formed into a keeled shape in flight

Juvenile

Natural Foods

Seeds and/or fruits of plants such as corn, oats, wheat, ragweed and blackberry; acorns; insects; crayfish; spiders; sow bugs; earthworms; snails

Feeder Fare

Sunflower seeds, suet, millet, peanuts, safflower seeds, fruits

Bird Brainy

Grackles are one of my favorite birds, but they aren't for everyone. A friend of mine who dislikes grackles took this photo and says it shows how evil they are! He sets this squirrel-proof feeder so that grackles are too heavy to feed from it. Unfortunately for him (and to my delight), his grackles have figured out that if they land on the feeder and fly upward while holding the perch with their feet, they can counterbalance the spring and get food out of the feeder. Birdbrains indeed!

Boat-tailed Grackle and Great-tailed Grackle

Quiscalus major and *Quiscalus mexicanus*

Male (*left*) and female (*right*) Boat-tailed Grackle

Male (*left*) and female (*right*) Great-tailed Grackle

ESSENTIALLY BIGGER VERSIONS of the Common Grackle, these more southern blackbirds are even more flamboyant with their colors and shapes. Great-tailed grackles are common across central and southwestern states, whereas Boat-tailed grackles are restricted to southeastern coasts and Florida. The two overlap in coastal Texas and western Louisiana, so extra care needs to be taken when identifying them in that region. Luckily, eye color can be helpful.

Natural Foods

Seeds and/or fruits of plants such as corn, rice, fig, grapes and berries; insects; spiders; crayfish; crabs; shrimp; small fish

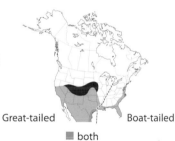

Great-tailed   Boat-tailed

■ both

Feeder Fare

Cracked corn, sunflower seeds

Pretty Posers

Blackbird family members are very talented at visual and auditory displays. Names for these displays include bill up (shown at left), ruff-out or song spread, bow, topple over, head-down, bill wipe, song flight, defense flutter, crouch and fluttering flight. Which blackbird displays can you see? Many of these displays are described in Birds of North America Online (birdsna.org). Are they directed at other males or at females? Did the display seem to work for the displayer?

BOAT-TAILED GRACKLE

Length: 16½ inches (42 cm), shorter than American Crow

Male is all black; female is brown overall

Eye: dark or sometimes dirty yellow in Florida and Gulf coast; yellow in Atlantic coast

Eyeline: dark on female

Beak: long, pointed

Head: iridescent blue on male, often very round

Body: iridescent greenish-blue on male

Wing: dark brown on female

Tail: long, may be formed into a keeled shape in flight; dark brown on female

GREAT-TAILED GRACKLE

Length: 18 inches (46 cm)

Male is all black; female is darker brown overall

Eyebrow: often paler on female

Eye: yellow; may be dark on juvenile and young female

Eyeline: dark on female

Beak: long, pointed

Head: iridescent blue on male, often very round

Body: often purplish iridescence

Wing: darker on female

Tail: very long, may be formed into a keeled shape in flight; dark brown on female

Orchard Oriole

(p. 268)

• Black head
• Rusty-orange shoulder
• Black back
• Rusty-orange
  underparts

Baltimore Oriole

(p. 266)

• Black head
• Orange shoulder
• Black back
• Bright orange
  underparts

Scott's Oriole

(p. 267)

• Black head
• Yellow shoulder
• Black back
• Yellow underparts

Audubon's Oriole

(southern Texas only)
(p. 283)

• Black head
• Green back
• Yellow underparts

Ornate Orioles

If your favorite color is orange, these are the birds for you! They are characterized by their long, pointed beak and, for the males, black and orange plumage. Many of the females are much duller overall and can be very tricky to identify, so beginners should try to focus on getting to know the males first.

Bullock's Oriole

(p. 266)

- Black eyeline
- Bright orange head and underparts
- Black throat
- Large white wing patch

Hooded Oriole

(p. 269)

- Black throat
- Bright orange head and underparts
- White shoulder patch

Spot-breasted Oriole

(Florida only) (p. 283)

- Bright orange head and underparts
- Black throat
- Black breast spots
- Black back

Altamira Oriole

(southern Texas only) (p. 283)

- Bright orange head and underparts
- Black throat
- Orange shoulder patch

Baltimore Oriole and Bullock's Oriole

Icterus galbula and *Icterus bullockii*

Adult male (*left*) and first-year female (*right*) Baltimore Oriole

Adult male (*left*) and first-year female (*right*) Bullock's Oriole

THESE TWO ARE the best known orioles across most of the lower 48 states and southern Canada. When I was a kid, they were called Baltimore and Bullock's Orioles. Then they were lumped together (see page 266), and for over a decade they were called the Northern Oriole. It took a long time to switch to using that name after learning the original names first. And now, since 1995, they are back to being the Baltimore Oriole and the Bullock's Oriole! I hope they don't ever switch back again . . .

Natural Foods
Insects; spiders; fruits of plants such as elderberry, fig, mulberry, serviceberry, cherry, grape, raspberry and blackberry; nectar

Feeder Fare
Fruits, jellies, sugar water, mealworms

Rock a Bye, Baby

The nests of Baltimore and Bullock's Orioles are some of the most recognizable in North America. A bag of woven plant fibers, strings and wool, it is built on the outer tips of branches of tall trees, where heavy predators can't reach. These orioles attach their nest firmly to these branches since winds can rock the nest quite violently at times, but the deep pocket keeps the eggs and/or young safely inside.

Length: 8¾ inches (22 cm), similar to Red-winged Blackbird

BALTIMORE ORIOLE

Male

Head and back: black

Underparts and rump: bright orange

Tail: black with bright orange outer feathers

Wing: black with orange and white wingbars

First-fall male is very similar to female

Female

Head and upperparts: variably mottled

Throat: possibly whitish

Wing: dark with white wingbars

Underparts, rump and tail: orange or yellow-orange

First-year female can have very gray upperparts, flanks and belly

BULLOCK'S ORIOLE

Male

Head: orange

Cap, eyeline, throat and back: black

Underparts and rump: bright orange

Tail: black with bright orange sides

Wing: black with white wing patch

Female and First-Year Male

Head, breast, rump and tail: yellowish-orange

Eyeline and throat: black on first-year male; no black on female

Upperparts: mottled

Belly and flanks: gray

Back: plain gray on female

Wing: white wingbars

Bullock's   Baltimore

Scott's Oriole

Icterus parisorum

Male

Female

A BIRD OF desert areas along mountain slopes and in valleys, the yellow plumage of the male Scott's Oriole easily sets it apart from most of our other north-of-Mexico orioles, which have orange plumage. This species builds a nest that is less bag-like and closer to the ground than Baltimore and Bullock's Orioles.

Natural Foods

Insects, spiders, small lizards, fruits, nectar

Feeder Fare

Fruits, jellies, sugar water, mealworms

Length: 9 inches (23 cm), similar to Red-winged Blackbird
MALE
Head, breast, back and tail: black
Shoulder: bright yellow
Wing: black with yellow and white wingbars
Underparts and rump: bright yellow
FEMALE
Head: brownish-gray
Back: mottled brown
Wing: dark with white wingbars
Underparts, rump and tail: yellowish
Throat, breast and face: may have some black; absent in first-year female, which is also less yellow overall

Bird–Plant Associations

Some birds depend heavily on certain plants for their survival — Pinyon Jays and pines, Acorn Woodpeckers and oaks, American Goldfinches and thistles. This association can be observed across their ranges or just in certain areas for certain populations. For example, some Scott's Oriole populations use yuccas extensively. They eat insects attracted to the yucca flowers and may eat the nectar as well. They also eat yucca moth caterpillars that eat the yucca seeds. Plus they can get moisture and nutrients from eating flower parts and fruit pods. They may even nest in the yucca.

Orchard Oriole

Icterus spurius

Adult male

Female

First-year male

THIS IS OUR smallest oriole. Its dark rusty-orange plumage helps distinguish it from the similarly marked Baltimore Oriole, which can nest in the same areas. The first-year male Orchard Oriole has a distinct black face and throat, which often confuses beginner birders because it looks like it may be some kind of large warbler species.

Natural Foods

Insects; fruits of plants such as mulberry, cherry, blackberry, blueberry and chokecherry; nectar

Feeder Fare

Fruits, jellies, sugar water, mealworms

Length: 7¼ inches (18.5 cm), similar to Brown-headed Cowbird
ADULT MALE
Head and back: black
Breast, underparts and rump: rusty-orange
Wing: orange and white wingbar
FEMALE AND FIRST-YEAR MALE
Face and throat: black on first-year male
Upperparts: olive-green
Underparts: yellow
Wing: white wingbars

Under the Protection of the King

Orchard Orioles have been known to nest near other bird species. If they nest near, for example, Eastern Kingbirds (shown here) or Western Kingbirds, they may get extra protection, since these species are very aggressive toward potential predators that get too close. Free bodyguards!

Hooded Oriole
Icterus cucullatus

Adult male

First-year male

Adult female

THIS MOSTLY MEXICAN oriole ranges into the southwestern states and much of California. It is found in scrubby areas, suburbs and deserts near water sources. The planting of palm trees in California likely helped Hooded Orioles expand their range northward along the coast.

Natural Foods
Insects, spiders, fruits, nectar

Feeder Fare
Fruits, jellies, sugar water, mealworms

Length: 8 inches (20.5 cm), similar to Red-winged Blackbird

ADULT MALE

Head: orange

Face and throat: black

Back and tail: black

Wing: black with white wingbars

Underparts and rump: orange

FEMALE AND FIRST-YEAR MALE

Head and underparts: yellow or light orange

Face and throat: black on first-year male; no black on female

Tail and rump: olive

Back: grayish

Wing: grayish with white wingbars

Female is duller overall, especially on upperparts

Bill Up
Early in the breeding season, Hooded Oriole males may be seen displaying the "bill up" posture at each other. This is an aggressive display and may attract other males, who may join in. Chasing and chattering may be part of the interactions as well.

More Feeder Birds

The birds on the following pages are either infrequent feeder visitors or have restricted ranges. If you see a strange bird at your feeder that you're having trouble identifying, flip through these pages, and you may find the species you're looking for.

It is also good to know about the feeder birds in places where you may be traveling. Who knows, maybe the place you are visiting will also have a bird feeder!

Northern Bobwhite

Colinus virginianus

THIS EASTERN QUAIL is known for its loud "Bob White!" call. A bird of farmland and scrubby areas, it is an uncommon visitor to feeders in the winter.

Length: 9¾ inches (25 cm), shorter than Rock Pigeon
Feeder Fare: cracked corn, millet, sunflower seeds

Male Northern Bobwhite

Female Northern Bobwhite

Montezuma Quail

Cyrtonyx montezumae

THIS LOCALIZED BIRD of the Southwest can be very hard to see. If you are lucky enough to have one show up at your feeder, you will notice the male's large black-and-white head.

Length: 8¾ inches (22 cm), shorter than Rock Pigeon
Feeder Fare: cracked corn, millet, sunflower seeds

Male Montezuma Quail

Female Montezuma Quail

Scaled Quail

Callipepla squamata

THIS SOUTH-CENTRAL quail has a light-colored tip on its crest and scaled breast feathers.

Length: 10 inches (25.5 cm), similar to American Robin
Feeder Fare: cracked corn, millet, sunflower seeds

Scaled Quail

Plain Chachalaca

Ortalis vetula

RESTRICTED TO EXTREME southern Texas, the large Plain Chachalaca is the only representative of its family found north of Mexico. More members are found in Central and South America.

Length: 22 inches (56 cm), longer than Red-tailed Hawk
Feeder Fare: cracked corn, fruits

Plain Chachalaca

Band-tailed Pigeon

Patagioenas fasciata

THIS WESTERN SPECIES is a forest bird, unlike many of North America's other dove and pigeon species, which prefer open habitats.

Length: 14½ inches (37 cm), longer than Rock Pigeon
Feeder Fare: cracked corn, sunflower seeds, millet

Band-tailed Pigeon

White-tipped Dove

Leptotila verreauxi

THIS DOVE IS found in extreme southern Texas. Watch for its white face and plain wings, which will help you distinguish it from the similar White-winged Dove.

Length: 11½ inches (29 cm), longer than Blue or Steller's Jay
Feeder Fare: cracked corn, millet, sunflower seeds

White-tipped Dove

Rivoli's Hummingbird

Eugenes fulgens

UNTIL RECENTLY, THIS large Southwestern hummer was called the Magnificent Hummingbird. Watch for the male's purple crown and green throat.

Length: 5¼ inches (13.5 cm), longer than Ruby-throated or Black-chinned Hummingbird
Feeder Fare: sugar water

Male Rivoli's Hummingbird

Blue-throated Hummingbird

Lampornis clemenciae

ANOTHER LARGE HUMMINGBIRD, this species is found in southeastern Arizona and southwestern Texas.

Length: 5 inches (13 cm), longer than Ruby-throated or Black-chinned Hummingbird
Feeder Fare: sugar water

Male Blue-throated Hummingbird

Broad-tailed Hummingbird

Selasphorus platycercus

THIS SPECIES IS similar to the Ruby-throated Hummingbird, but it has a pinker-red throat and does not have a black mask. It breeds in the central to southwestern states.

Length: 4 inches (10 cm), longer than Ruby-throated or Black-chinned Hummingbird
Feeder Fare: sugar water

Male Broad-tailed Hummingbird

Calliope Hummingbird

Selasphorus calliope

THIS IS THE smallest hummingbird north of Mexico. It is found in the western states and northward, all the way to the middle of British Columbia.

Length: 3¼ inches (8 cm), shorter than Ruby-throated or Black-chinned Hummingbird
Feeder Fare: sugar water

Male Calliope Hummingbird

Violet-crowned Hummingbird

Amazilia violiceps

THE VIOLET-CROWNED Hummingbird just makes it into the United States, breeding in southeastern Arizona and southwestern New Mexico.

Length: 4½ inches (11.5 cm), longer than Ruby-throated or Black-chinned Hummingbird
Feeder Fare: sugar water

Male Violet-crowned Hummingbird

Buff-bellied Hummingbird

Amazilia yucatanensis

THIS HUMMER IS found in the extreme southern tip of Texas in the summer and the southern parts of Louisiana and east Texas in the winter.

Length: 4 inches (10 cm), longer than Ruby-throated or Black-chinned Hummingbird
Feeder Fare: sugar water

Male Buff-bellied Hummingbird

Broad-billed Hummingbird

Cynanthus latirostris

THE MALE OF this species can be recognized by its deep blue throat and forehead and dark green upperparts. Watch for its orange beak as well. It is found in southeastern Arizona.

Length: 4 inches (10 cm), longer than Ruby-throated or Black-chinned Hummingbird
Feeder Fare: sugar water

Male Broad-billed Hummingbird

Costa's Hummingbird

Calypte costae

THE SMALL COSTA'S Hummingbird has a deep purple throat with flared edges. It is found in the deserts of southern California and Arizona.

Length: 3½ inches (9 cm), shorter than Ruby-throated or Black-chinned Hummingbird
Feeder Fare: sugar water

Male Costa's Hummingbird

Lewis's Woodpecker

Melanerpes lewis

THE GLOSSY PLUMAGE of this woodpecker is quite distinctive. It is found north of Mexico in the western United States and in southern British Columbia.

Length: 10¼ inches (26 cm), longer than Hairy Woodpecker
Feeder Fare: suet, suet/peanut butter spread, peanuts

Lewis's Woodpecker

Gilded Flicker

Colaptes chrysoides

SEPARATE THIS SOUTHWESTERN flicker from the Northern Flicker by looking for its brown cap, gray face and, for males, a combination of a red moustache and yellow flight feathers.

Length: 11 inches (28 cm), longer than Hairy Woodpecker
Feeder Fare: suet, suet/peanut butter spread, peanuts, fruits

Male Gilded Flicker

Gila Woodpecker

Melanerpes uropygialis

THE MALE OF this desert species is differentiated from the female by the red patch on the top of his head.

Length: 9¼ inches (23.5 cm), similar to Hairy Woodpecker
Feeder Fare: suet, suet/peanut butter spread, fruits, sugar water

Male Gila Woodpecker

Golden-fronted Woodpecker

Melanerpes aurifrons

THIS WOODPECKER IS restricted to central Texas. Females lack the red crown patch but still have the golden patches.

Length: 9½ inches (24 cm), similar to Hairy Woodpecker
Feeder Fare: suet, suet/peanut butter spread, peanuts, sunflower seeds, fruits, sugar water

Male Golden-fronted Woodpecker

White-headed Woodpecker

Dryobates albolarvatus

LIKE MANY WOODPECKERS, the only difference between the males and females of this western species is the lack of red on the female's head.

Length: 9¼ inches (23.5 cm), similar to Hairy Woodpecker
Feeder Fare: suet, suet/peanut butter spread

Male
White-headed
Woodpecker

Arizona Woodpecker

Dryobates arizonae

ONCE CALLED THE Brown-backed Woodpecker, this species looks very much like a brown version of the Hairy Woodpecker. It is found in southeastern Arizona.

Length: 7½ inches (19 cm), longer than Downy Woodpecker
Feeder Fare: suet, suet/peanut butter spread

Male Arizona
Woodpecker

Ladder-backed Woodpecker

Dryobates scalaris

A SMALL WOODPECKER of the southwestern United States, this bird prefers dry woods and desert scrub.

Length: 7¼ inches (18.5 cm), longer than Downy Woodpecker
Feeder Fare: suet, suet/peanut butter spread, sunflower seeds, peanuts, sugar water

Male
Ladder-backed
Woodpecker

Nuttall's Woodpecker

Dryobates nuttallii

FOUND ONLY IN California and adjacent Mexico, the Nuttall's Woodpecker is similar to the Ladder-backed Woodpecker, but it has more black on its cheeks and upper back.

Length: 7½ inches (19 cm), longer than Downy Woodpecker
Feeder Fare: suet, suet/peanut butter spread, sunflower seeds

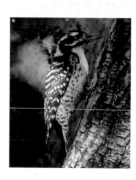

Male Nuttall's
Woodpecker

Black Phoebe

Sayornis nigricans

THIS BLACK-AND-white flycatcher is found on the U.S. West Coast and the states that border Mexico.

Length: 7 inches (18 cm), shorter than Brown-headed Cowbird
Feeder Fare: possibly suet/peanut butter spread, mealworms

Black Phoebe

Eastern Phoebe

Sayornis phoebe

THIS IS USUALLY the first flycatcher seen in the spring in the Northeast, where it may be attracted to flies warming up on the sunny walls of buildings.

Length: 7 inches (18 cm), shorter than Brown-headed Cowbird
Feeder Fare: possibly suet/peanut butter spread, mealworms

Eastern Phoebe

Say's Phoebe

Sayornis saya

LOOK FOR THE lovely orangish wash on the belly and undertail coverts of this phoebe.

Length: 7½ inches (19 cm), similar to Brown-headed Cowbird
Feeder Fare: possibly suet/peanut butter spread, mealworms

Say's Phoebe

Horned Lark

Eremophila alpestris

THIS IS A bird of open fields. If you live in farmland, you may be able to attract Horned Larks during the winter by spreading cracked corn on the ground.

Length: 7¼ inches (18.5 cm), similar to Brown-headed Cowbird
Feeder Fare: cracked corn

Horned Lark

Green Jay

Cyanocorax yncas

SOUTHERN TEXAS IS where you can find this tropical-looking jay. They often gather in small flocks.

Length: 10½ inches (27 cm), shorter than Blue or Steller's Jay
Feeder Fare: suet/peanut butter spread, sunflower seeds, fruits

Green Jay

Mexican Jay

Aphelocoma wollweberi

THIS RELATIVE OF the scrub-jays is found in southeastern Arizona, southwestern New Mexico and southwestern Texas.

Length: 11½ inches (29 cm), similar to Blue or Steller's Jay
Feeder Fare: suet/peanut butter spread, peanuts

Mexican Jay

Bridled Titmouse

Baeolophus wollweberi

THIS STRIKING TITMOUSE has a restricted range and is found only in central and southeastern Arizona and southwestern New Mexico.

Length: 5¼ inches (13.5 cm), similar to Black-capped Chickadee
Feeder Fare: sunflower seeds, safflower seeds, peanuts, suet, suet/peanut butter spread, mealworms

Bridled Titmouse

House Wren

Troglodytes aedon

THIS SPECIES IS found across the United States and southern Canada. The best way to attract it to your yard is with a bird box (see pages 64–69).

Length: 4¾ inches (12 cm), shorter than Black-capped Chickadee
Feeder Fare: suet/peanut butter spread, mealworms

House Wren

Green-tailed Towhee

Pipilo chlorurus

OUR ONLY GREENISH towhee, this western species may be attracted to seed spread on the ground in a spot with lots of cover.

Length: 7¼ inches (18.5 cm), similar to Brown-headed Cowbird
Feeder Fare: millet, sunflower seeds, cracked corn

Green-tailed Towhee

Abert's Towhee

Melozone aberti

ITS DARK FACE and pale beak help separate this towhee from California and Canyon Towhees. It is restricted to the southwestern United States.

Length: 9½ inches (24 cm), shorter than American Robin
Feeder Fare: millet, sunflower seeds, cracked corn

Abert's Towhee

Snow Bunting

Plectrophenax nivalis

THIS BIRD OF the Far North visits mid-latitude North American fields in the winter. Huge winter flocks of hundreds of birds can be found in snowy, windswept farm fields, but it is uncommon at feeders.

Length: 6¾ inches (17 cm), similar to Downy Woodpecker
Feeder Fare: cracked corn, millet

Summer male Snow Bunting (*left*)
Winter Snow Bunting (*right*)

Lapland Longspur

Calcarius lapponicus

ANOTHER BIRD OF the tundra, Lapland Longspurs can sometimes be found within large flocks of Snow Buntings.

Length: 6¼ inches (16 cm), similar to Dark-eyed Junco
Feeder Fare: cracked corn, millet

Summer male Lapland Longspur (*left*)
Winter Lapland Longspur (*right*)

Yellow-eyed Junco

Junco phaeonotus

EXCEPT FOR ITS bright yellow eyes, this junco is very similar to the Dark-eyed Junco. It is found in southeast Arizona.

Length: 6¼ inches (16 cm), similar to Dark-eyed Junco
Feeder Fare: millet, sunflower seeds, cracked corn

Yellow-eyed Junco

Eurasian Tree Sparrow

Passer montanus

THIS SPARROW WAS introduced in St. Louis, Missouri, in 1870, and its range hasn't expanded very far. The brown cap and black cheek patch will help you differentiate it from a male House Sparrow.

Length: 6 inches (15 cm), shorter than Dark-eyed Junco
Feeder Fare: millet, sunflower seeds, cracked corn

Eurasian Tree Sparrow

Dickcissel

Spiza americana

A BIRD OF open fields, it is not a common feeder visitor but may show up within a flock of House Sparrows.

Length: 6¼ inches (16 cm), similar to Dark-eyed Junco
Feeder Fare: millet, cracked corn

Male Dickcissel (*left*)
First-winter Dickcissel (*right*)

Varied Bunting

Passerina versicolor

THE MALE OF this species is a lovely blend of rosy-pink and purplish-blue. It is found only in southern Texas and southern Arizona.

Length: 5½ inches (14 cm), longer than Black-capped Chickadee
Feeder Fare: millet, sunflower seeds

Male Varied Bunting (*left*)
Female Varied Bunting (*right*)

Clay-colored Sparrow

Spizella pallida

WATCH FOR THIS small sparrow's brown cheek patch surrounded by a gray eyeline and gray nape, and listen for its buzzy song.

Length: 5½ inches (14 cm), shorter than Dark-eyed Junco
Feeder Fare: millet, sunflower seeds, cracked corn

Clay-colored Sparrow

Brewer's Sparrow

Spizella breweri

THIS SMALL, NONDESCRIPT sparrow has a fairly plain face and a white eyering. It is a western bird and prefers scrubby areas.

Length: 5½ inches (14 cm), shorter than Dark-eyed Junco
Feeder Fare: millet, sunflower seeds, cracked corn

Brewer's Sparrow

Savannah Sparrow

Passerculus sandwichensis

THIS SPECIES IS similar to a Song Sparrow. Watch for its yellow lores and short tail. Different subspecies can be redder, darker or lighter than others.

Length: 5½ inches (14 cm), shorter than Dark-eyed Junco
Feeder Fare: millet, sunflower seeds, cracked corn

Savannah Sparrow

Lincoln's Sparrow

Melospiza lincolni

A CLOSE RELATIVE of the Song Sparrow, the Lincoln's Sparrow has thin, dark breast streaks on a creamy background and a wide gray eyeline.

Length: 5¾ inches (14.5 cm), shorter than Dark-eyed Junco
Feeder Fare: millet, sunflower seeds, cracked corn

Lincoln's Sparrow

Lark Sparrow

Chondestes grammacus

THE COLORFUL HEAD pattern of the Lark Sparrow helps distinguish it from all the other sparrows that may show up at your feeder.

Length: 6½ inches (16.5 cm), slightly longer than Dark-eyed Junco
Feeder Fare: millet, sunflower seeds, cracked corn, suet/peanut butter spread

Lark Sparrow

Rufous-crowned Sparrow

Aimophila ruficeps

A BIRD OF the Southwest, this uncommon feeder visitor has a white eyering, white moustache and rufous cap.

Length: 6 inches (15 cm), slightly shorter than Dark-eyed Junco
Feeder Fare: millet

Rufous-crowned Sparro

Rufous-winged Sparrow

Peucaea carpalis

THIS SPECIES IS restricted to extreme south-central Arizona and is found in dry grasslands.

Length: 5¾ inches (14.5 cm), shorter than Dark-eyed Junco
Feeder Fare: millet

Rufous-winged Sparrow

Black-throated Sparrow

Amphispiza bilineata

ANOTHER SOUTHWESTERN SPECIES, the Black-throated Sparrow is found in dry, scrubby areas. Its lovely face pattern makes it an easy sparrow to identify.

Length: 5½ inches (14.5 cm), shorter than Dark-eyed Junco
Feeder Fare: millet, nyjer

Black-throated Sparrow

Palm Warbler

Setophaga palmarum

THOUGH IT BREEDS in northern bogs and open brush, this warbler may spend its winter foraging on lawns in the Southeast. Watch for its distinctive tail pumping.

Length: 5½ inches (14 cm), similar to Black-capped Chickadee
Feeder Fare: sunflower seeds, possibly other seeds

Winter Palm Warbler

Black-throated Gray Warbler

Setophaga nigrescens

THE ONLY COLOR on this monochromatic western warbler is the yellow spot on its lore. Its appearance is almost chickadee-like.

Length: 5 inches (13 cm), similar to Black-capped Chickadee
Feeder Fare: suet, suet/peanut butter spread

Male Black-throated Gray Warbler (*left*)
Female Black-throated Gray Warbler (*right*)

Townsend's Warbler

Setophaga townsendi

THIS COLORFUL WARBLER is yellow, black, green and white. It breeds in the Northwest, and some winter along the U.S. West Coast.

Length: 5 inches (13 cm), similar to Black-capped Chickadee
Feeder Fare: suet, suet/peanut butter spread, mealworms

Male Townsend's Warbler (*left*)
Female Townsend's Warbler (*right*)

Bronzed Cowbird

Molothrus aeneus

FOUND IN THE southern areas of the states that border Mexico, this cowbird is longer and heavier than its brown-headed cousin.

Length: 8¾ inches (22 cm), similar to Red-winged Blackbird
Feeder Fare: seeds

Male Bronzed Cowbird (*left*)
Female Bronzed Cowbird (*right*)

Yellow-headed Blackbird

Xanthocephalus xanthocephalus

THE MALE'S BRIGHT yellow head and black body make it unmistakable. It is not as common at feeders as many of the other blackbird species.

Length: 9½ inches (24 cm), shorter than American Robin
Feeder Fare: cracked corn, millet, sunflower seeds

Male Yellow-headed Blackbird (*left*)
Female Yellow-headed Blackbird (*right*)

Altamira Oriole

Icterus gularis

A LARGE AND bright oriole of extreme southern Texas, the Altamira Oriole is a treat for those who can attract one to their feeders.

Length: 10 inches (25.5 cm), similar to American Robin
Feeder Fare: fruits, jellies, sugar water

Adult Altamira Oriole (*left*)
First-year Altamira Oriole (*right*)

Spot-breasted Oriole

Icterus pectoralis

THIS ORIOLE WAS introduced to southeastern Florida from Mexico, and it is not found elsewhere in the United States or in Canada.

Length: 9½ inches (24 cm), shorter than American Robin
Feeder Fare: fruits, jellies, sugar water

Spot-breasted Oriole

Audubon's Oriole

Icterus graduacauda

THE AUDUBON'S ORIOLE is found in extreme southern Texas. It is yellow like the Scott's Oriole, but it has a greenish, not black, back.

Length: 9½ inches (24 cm), shorter than American Robin
Feeder Fare: fruits, jellies, sugar water

Audubon's Oriole

California Thrasher

Toxostoma redivivum

TRUE TO ITS name, the California Thrasher is found in both the state of California and Baja California.

Length: 12 inches (30.5 cm), longer than Blue or Steller's Jay
Feeder Fare: suet, fruits, seeds

California Thrasher

Long-billed Thrasher

Toxostoma longirostre

THIS STREAKY THRASHER is only found in southern Texas.

Length: 11½ inches (29 cm), longer than Blue or Steller's Jay
Feeder Fare: seeds

Long-billed Thrasher

Crissal Thrasher

Toxostoma crissale

THE EXTREMELY CURVED beak, white moustache and rusty undertail coverts of this thrasher will help you identify it. It is found in dry areas of the Southwest.

Length: 11.5 inches (29 cm), longer than Blue or Steller's Jay
Feeder Fare: seeds

Crissal Thrasher

Hepatic Tanager

Piranga flava

THIS TANAGER SPECIES is restricted to Arizona, New Mexico and western Texas.

Length: 8 inches (20.5 cm), longer than Brown-headed Cowbird
Feeder Fare: suet, fruits, jellies, some seeds

Male Hepatic Tanager (*left*)
Female Hepatic Tanager (*right*)

Raptors and Shrikes

Many of these species have wide ranges and are found in many places in North America.

Sharp-shinned Hawk

Accipiter striatus

LITTLE BIRDS BEWARE! This predator catches its avian prey through fast, surprise attacks. As described by Studer, "Its flight is peculiar — swift, spirited, and irregular . . . it seems to advance by sudden dashes, and when once its prey is discovered, will pounce upon it with a swiftness which makes escape impossible" (1881).

Adult

Immature

Length:
Male: 10 inches (26 cm), similar to American Robin
Female: 12½ inches (32 cm), similar to Rock Dove
Head: small, dove-like, red eye
Breast and belly: white with thick rusty-orange barring
Back and wings: bluish-gray, may have white spots on back; female may be brownish-gray
Tail: squarish, bluish-gray with thick dark bands and thin white terminal band; from below, the tail feathers appear to be roughly the same length
Undertail coverts: white
First year is similar to adult, except eyes are yellow, upperparts are brown, and breast and belly are whitish with thick brown streaks

Cooper's Hawk

Accipiter cooperii

THIS IS THE mid-size model of our three hawks from the genus *Accipiter*. The wings and tail of a Cooper's Hawk are proportionally longer than that of the Sharp-shinned Hawk or goshawk. Cooper's Hawks usually focus on larger prey than Sharp-shinned Hawks. They may take Rock Doves right above busy city streets.

Adult

Immature

Length:
Male: 15 inches (39 cm), shorter than American Crow
Female: 17½ inches (45 cm), similar to American Crow
Head: largish, may have a darkish cap
Eye: red
Breast and belly: white with thick rusty-orange bars
Back and wings: bluish-gray, may have white spots on back; female may be brownish-gray
Tail: rounded, bluish-gray with thick, dark bands and white terminal band; when viewing from below, you can see shorter outer tail feathers
Undertail coverts: white
First year is similar to adult except that eyes are yellow, upperparts are brown, and breast and upper belly are whitish with thin brown streaks

Northern Goshawk

Accipiter gentilis

"THE GOSHAWK [is] one of the deadliest, handsomest, bravest birds of prey in the world." So wrote Sass in 1930 (in Bent, 1968), and if you have ever been near an active goshawk nest, then you know this is true! They are very protective of their nestlings.

Adult

Immature

Length:
Male: 21½ inches (55 cm), similar to Red-tailed Hawk
Female: 24 inches (61 cm), longer than Red-tailed Hawk
Head: small; dark cap, red eye
Eyeline: dark
Eyebrow: thick, white
Breast and belly: white with very thin gray barring
Back and wing: bluish-gray; female may be brownish gray
Tail: bluish-gray with thick, dark bands
Undertail coverts: white
First year is similar to adult except that eyes are yellow; upperparts are brown but may have some white spotting; underparts are whitish with thick brown streaks, including some streaks on the undertail coverts; tail has thick, dark and jagged bands, and each tail band has a thin, light border on its upper surface

Peregrine Falcon

Falco peregrinus

THIS FALCON IS estimated to go as fast as 225 miles per hour (360 km/h) when it is diving down onto its prey, making it the fastest animal on Earth. It has been known to catch everything from tiny hummingbirds to huge cranes and geese.

Adult

Immature

Length:
Male: 17 inches (43 cm), similar to American Crow
Female: 20½ inches (52 cm), similar to Red-tailed Hawk
Cap: black
Moustache: black
Cheek and throat: white
Underparts: light with dark barring
Back and wings: dark gray
Tail: gray with narrow, dark bands
Undertail coverts: light with dark barring
First year is similar to adult except that crown is brown or buffy; moustache is dark; dark patch around eye; back is brown; underparts are buffy or whitish with dark streaks; tail is brown with dark, narrow bands

Merlin

Falco columbarius

THE MERLIN MAY be little, but it is an unforgiving predator of small birds. Merlins often hunt by perching near an open field or small lake and waiting for a small bird to cross. It then chases down its meal with an impressive burst of speed.

Length: 10 inches (25.5 cm), similar to American Robin

Head and upperparts: Dark to light gray

Underparts: pale rufous to whitish with dark streaks (lighter overall in the Prairies, much darker overall on the West Coast)

Moustache: dusky, indistinct

Tail: thick, dark bands, usually separated with narrow, light bands

Adult eastern female and first year are similar to adult male but have browner upperparts

American Kestrel

Falco sparverius

OUR SMALLEST AND most colorful raptor has a special hunting style that is not often used by other birds of prey: it hovers in place, facing the wind, which allows it to see and then drop onto an unsuspecting meadow vole or grasshopper.

Male

Female

Length: 9 inches (23 cm), shorter than American Robin

Cap: bluish-gray with a rufous central spot on male; gray on female

Head: two large black spots on the back on male; more subdued pattern on female

Face: thick black moustache and sideburns

Back: rufous with dark barring

Wing: bluish-gray with black spots on male; rufous with dark barring on female

Breast: pale rufous blending to white undertail coverts on male; all white with rufous streaks on female

Belly: pale rufous with black spots on male; white with rufous streaks on female

Tail: long and narrow, rufous; male has white outer tail feathers that might have dark spots, thin, white terminal band, thick black subterminal band; female has dark narrow bands, often pumps tail up and down

Loggerhead Shrike

Lanius excubitor

THIS IS A songbird that acts like a hawk. Shrikes prey on small rodents, small birds, lizards, frogs, spiders, beetles, grasshoppers and other insects. They catch their food with their strong beak and may use their feet to help carry heavy prey. To rip up their prey, they hang it on thorns or other sharp objects that hold it still while they tear at it with their beak.

Length: 9 inches (23 cm), shorter than American Robin
Mask: black
Beak: black, hooked
Upperparts: gray
Underparts: whitish
Wing: black with white flashes
Tail: black with white outer tips
Immature is brownish with faint barring overall

Northern Shrike

Lanius ludovicianus

THIS LARGE SHRIKE breeds across northern boreal and southern tundra borderlands in both North America and Asia. Our continent's population can often be found in southern Canada and the northern states during the winter, where they can be seen hunting small birds at feeders.

Length: 10 inches (25.5 cm), similar to American Robin
Mask: black, thinner than Loggerhead
Beak: black, hooked, often with a lighter base on lower mandible
Upperparts: gray
Underparts: whitish
Wing: black with white flashes
Tail: black with white outer tips
Immature is brownish with faint barring overall

Birds at My Feeder List

Use this chart to get yourself started on making your very own feeder bird list then expand it into a journal or notebook. You may be surprised by the number of species you record as time goes by! Use the notes section to write down interesting behaviors, foods eaten, numbers, weather and/or who saw the bird with you.

BIRD	DATE	NOTES

Works Cited

Audubon, John James. *John James Audubon: Writings and Drawings*. New York, NY: Library of America, 1999.

Bent, Arthur Cleveland. *Life Histories of North American Cardinals, Grosbeaks, Buntings, Towhees, Finches, Sparrows, and Allies*. 3 parts. Compiled and edited by Oliver L. Austin, Jr. Washington, DC: U.S. National Museum, 1968.

Chapman, F.M. *The Warblers of North America*. New York, NY: D. Appleton and Company, 1907.

Dillard, Annie. *Pilgrim at Tinker Creek*. New York, NY: Harper & Row, 1974.

Forbush, E.H. *Birds of Massachusetts and Other New England States*. Norwood, MA: Norwood Press, 1929.

McNicholl, John L., and Martin K. Cranmer-Byng, eds. *Ornithology in Ontario*. Whitby, ON: Hawk Owl Publishing, 1994.

Studer, Jacob H. *Studer's Popular Ornithology: The Birds of North America*. N.p.: Harrison House, 1881.

Thoreau, Henry David. *Thoreau on Birds: Notes on New England Birds from the Journals of Henry David Thoreau*. Boston, MA: Beacon Press, 1910.

Further Reading

Barker, Margaret, and Elissa Wolfson. *Audubon Birdhouse Book*. Minneapolis, MN: Voyageur Press, 2013.

Barker, Margaret, and Jack Griggs. *A Cornell Bird Library Guide: The Feederwatcher's Guide to Bird Feeding*. New York, NY: HarperCollins Publishers Inc., 2000.

Carpenter, Jim. *The Joy of Bird Feeding*. New York, NY: Scott and Nix Inc., 2017.

Dunn, Erica, and Dianne Tessaglia-Hymes. *Birds at Your Feeder*. New York, NY: Norton and Company, 1999.

Earley, Chris. *Hawks and Owls of Eastern North America*. Richmond Hill. ON: Firefly Books Ltd., 2012.

Earley, Chris. *Sparrows and Finches of the Great Lakes Region and Eastern North America*. Richmond Hill, ON: Firefly Books Ltd., 2003.

Earley, Chris. *Warblers of the Great Lakes Region and Eastern North America*. Richmond Hill, ON: Firefly Books Ltd., 2003.

Sibley, David A. *The Sibley Guide to Bird Life and Behavior*. New York, NY: Alfred A. Knopf, 2001.

Stokes, Donald and Lillian. *Stokes Nature Guides: Bird Behavior*. 3 vols. Boston, MA: Little, Brown and Company, 1979–89.

Tallamy, Douglas. *Bringing Nature Home*. Portland, OR: Timber Press, 2007.

Photo Credits

Interior:
Photos © Chris Earley, except as specified below.

Alexandra Kocher: 162 (bottom box, top inset and bottom inset); Aurora Santiago: 94 (top); barb biagi: 214 (bottom); Brenda Doherty: 66, 286 (top left); Brett Forsyth Photography – brettforsyth.com: 167 (bottom), 168 (center left); Brian E. Small: 134 (1st row, 4th), 134 (4th row, 2nd), 134 (9th row, 3rd), 135 (1st row, 1st and 2nd), 135 (6th row, 2nd), 135 (10th row, 2nd), 136 (top row, 3rd), 138 (center row, right), 147 (bottom), 148 (bottom), 150 (bottom), 153 (center left), 154 (top right), 155 (top row, 1st and 2nd), 161 (top row, right), 161 (center row, right), 166 (top row, 3rd), 168 (center right), 169 (top), 177 (top row, 4th), 181 (top row, 4th), 182 (top right and top left), 194 (center row, left), 203 (center right), 203 (top), 205 (top row, left), 207 (bottom row, 4th), 208 (bottom row, 1st, 2nd and 3rd), 209, (top row, 4th), 211 (top row, 1st, 2nd, 3rd and 4th), 219 (top row, 4th), 220 (top right), 223 (top row, 2nd), 224 (top right), 230 (bottom row, 3rd), 232 (top row, 3rd), 237 (top row, right), 237 (2nd row, right), 238 (top row, 3rd and 4th), 238 (bottom row, 2nd and 4th), 244 (top row, 2nd), 246 (top row, left), 251 (bottom row, 1st and 2nd), 255 (top row, 2nd, 3rd and 4th), 256 (top row, 3rd), 256 (bottom row, 4th), 261 (top row, 2nd and 3rd), 264 (top row, 3rd), 266 (top row, right), 267 (top right and left), 270 (3rd and 4th), 274 (2nd), 278 (2nd), 279 (3rd row, right), 279 (4th row, right and left), 282 (3rd row, left), 284 (3rd), 284 (4th row, right and left); Catherine, The Herb Lady, Crowley: 146 (bottom); Clive Dobson: 26 (bottom); Daniel Arndt: 197 (bottom left); Daybreak Imagery / Kimball Stock: 42 (top right), 42 (bottom), 43 (top), 69 (top left and right); Debbie Oppermann: 117 (bottom); Deborah E. Bifulco: 31 (bottom left); Denny Granstrand: 211 (bottom); Don Delaney, Edmonta, Alberta: 287 (top right); Ed Peachey: 237 (bottom left); Ian MacDonald: 187 (bottom), 262 (bottom); Janet Forjan: 229 (bottom), 234 (bottom); Jason Taylor: 180 (bottom left); Jean Iron: 220 (center row, 2nd, 3rd and 4th); John Breitsch: 237 (2nd row, center); Justin Peter: 246 (2nd row, center); Karl Egressy: 57 (bottom), 110 (top), 158 (bottom right), 197 (center), 216 (2nd row, center), 228 (top row, 1st), 230 (top row, 3rd), 230 (bottom row, 2nd), 232 (top row, 1st), 236 (top), 236 (center right), 238 (top row, 1st), 238 (bottom row, 1st); Kelly Balkom: 213 (bottom); Larry Keller – Lititz, PA: 64; Marie Read: 54 (bottom), 57 (top), 77 (bottom), 93 (top center), 109, 127, 130, 136 (bottom), 139 (top left and bottom), 161 (bottom box, top left, bottom left and right), 169 (right), 172 (bottom right), 178 (bottom), 182 (bottom), 188 (bottom left), 190 (bottom), 198 (bottom), 201 (bottom), 204 (bottom left), 206 (bottom left), 207 (top row, 2nd), 216 (bottom right), 216 (2nd row, left), 217 (bottom); Mark T. O'Neill: 25; Melanie Howarth: 16, 56 (bottom), 58 (all), 59, 60, 94 (bottom), 97 (top), 104 (bottom), 105 (top and center), 113 (center left), 114 (bottom right), 123 (center right), 185 (bottom), 222 (bottom), 224 (bottom), 251 (bottom row, 3rd), 256 (top row, 2nd), 259 (bottom), 260 (top right); Paul Bannick / PaulBannick.com: 158 (left); Robert McCaw: 76 (left and right), 173 (bottom), 181, (center); Roger Mayhorn – Buchanan County, VA: 202 (bottom); Skye Earley: 45 (bottom left); Steven Lospalluto / Dunbar Gardens: 36 (top), 54 (top left); Stuart McCausland: 225 (bottom); Tom Davenport: 184 (bottom); Tom Vaughan / FeVa Fotos: 113 (center right).

Alamy
Bernard Friel / DanitaDelimont.com: 250 (bottom), 254 (bottom left); BRIAN E SMALL / Nature Photographers Ltd: 219 (top row, 5th); Cal Vornberger: 164 (right); Genevieve Vallee: 267 (bottom); Johann Schumacher: 125 (bottom); John MacTavish: 122 (top right); Rolf Nussbaumer Photography: 177 (bottom).

First Light
Don Johnston: 71; FLPA/S & D & K Maslow: 27 (bottom), 35 (center left), 39; FOTOSEARCH RM: 70 (bottom); J & C Sohns: 117 (center); Rolf Nussbaumer / imageBROKER: 245 (top row, 3rd), 246 (2nd row, right).

Minden Pictures
Alan Murphy: 212 (top row, 2nd); Donald M. Jones: 212 (bottom); Espen Bergensen: 175 (bottom); R and M Van Nostrand: 219 (center).

Nature Picture Library
Barry Mansell: 177 (bottom row, 4th), 186 (top right); David Welling: 269 (top center), 279 (1st); Floris van Breugel: 151 (bottom), 155 (bottom); Gerrit Vyn: 176 (bottom row, 2nd), 242 (bottom), 261 (bottom left); Rolf Nussbaumer: 92 (top), 254 (2nd row, center).

Shutterstock
aaltair: 173 (top row, center); Adam Fichna: 119 (bottom); Adrian Burke: 263 (top row, 2nd); Agami Photo Agency: 112; Agnieszka Bacal: 243 (bottom), 255 (bottom); Aika Estelle: 99 (bottom stacked, top); Al Mueller: 207 (bottom row, 1st); anaisanais: 223 (bottom), 227 (bottom); Anatoliy Lukich: 32 (center), 34 (top), 171 (left stacked, top) 251 (top row, 2nd and 3rd), 253 (top center); Andrew M. Allport: 143 (top row, 2nd), 145 (top left); Angel DiBilio: 257 (bottom row, 3rd); Anze Furlan: 210 (bottom); Ariel Celeste Photography: 247 (center right); Arto Hakola: 134 (8th row, 4th), 149 (bottom), 198 (top row, 2nd), 201 (top right), 263 (top row, 1st); Avik: 33 (top right); Bachkova Natalia: 134 (10th row, 3rd), 199 (top row, 2nd), 204 (center right);

Becky Swora: 157 (1st); BestPhotoStudio: 204 (bottom row, left); Betty Shelton: 137 (top row, 2nd), 141 (right stacked, top); BGSmith: 167 (top row, 4th); Birdiegal: 134 (6th row, 2nd), 192 (center right), 207 (bottom row, 2nd), 219 (top row 1st), 276 (1st); Birds and Dragons: 143 (bottom row, 2nd), 148 (top), 275 (3rd); Bobby Dailey: 33 (top center); Bonnie Taylor Barry: 38 (bottom stacked, bottom), 96 (center left), 134 (6th row, 4th), 189 (top row 3rd), 194 (top center), 208 (bottom row 4th), 218 (2nd row, left), 230 (top row, 1st), 235 (top center), 245 (top row, 4th), 246 (top row, right), 251 (bottom row, 4th), 254 (top row, center and right), 257 (bottom row, 4th); Brian E Kushner: 122 (bottom left), 196 (top center), 222 (top row, 2nd), 226 (top row, 5th), 240 (top right); Brian Lasenby: 33 (top left), 135 (8th row, 4th), 143 (top row, 3rd), 146 (top right), 156 (1st and 3rd), 158 (center right), 172 (bottom left), 246 (bottom), 258 (top left); Bruce MacQueen: 134 (3rd row, 3rd), 160 (center row, left), 176 (top row, 2nd), 178 (top left); ChameleonsEye: 45 (top left); Charles Brutlag: 201 (top left), 254 (2nd row, right), 276 (2nd); Charles Knowles: 70 (top left); Chesapeake Images: 68, 226 (top row, 3rd), 268 (top right); Chris Hill: 31 (bottom center), 135 (8th row, 1st), 208 (top row, 1st), 213 (top right), 230 (bottom row, 1st), 236 (bottom row, 3rd), 239 (top left), 287 (bottom left); Christopher P McLeod: 102; cindylindowphotography: 288 (bottom right); Collins 93: 250 (top row, 4th), 254 (top row, left); Dan Logan: 164 (2nd row, right), 265 (bottom), 266 (bottom left); Daniel Hebert: 199 (top row, 3rd), 231 (top row, 3rd), 240 (top left); Danita Delmont: 226 (bottom box, right), 269)(top right), 271 (1st); David Byron Keener: 47, 55 (center right), 240 (bottom box, 2nd from the top); David W. Leindecker: 162 (center row, right); Dec Hogan: 150 (top row, 1st and 3rd), 153 (top left), 272 (3rd); DeltaSierra: 245 (bottom row, 4th), 248 (top center); Dennis Jacobsen: 123 (bottom left), 145 (top right), 209 (bottom row, 3rd), 210 (top row, left), 276 (4th); Dennis Von Linden: 29 (bottom left); Dennis W Donohue: 120 (bottom right), 134 (10th row, 4th), 151 (top row, 4th), 183 (center left), 205 (top row, center), 233 (bottom), 242 (top center), 249 (bottom center), 273 (3rd); devonx: 144 (bottom right stacked, top); Diana Carpenter: 253 (top right), 282 (bottom row, left); Dietlinde B. DuPlessis: 274 (3rd), 277 (1st); dimostudio: 166 (top row, 2nd); Dmitry Polonskiy: 134 (3rd row, 1st), 144 (top); Don Fink: 245 (top row, 1st), 247 (top row, center); Don Flamingo: 90 (bottom); Don Mammoser: 170 (top center), 215 (bottom box, center row, right), 215 (top left), 283 (top row, right), 288 (bottom left); Double Brow Imagery: 230 (top row, 2nd), 235 (top left); Ed Schneider: 146 (4th), 161 (center row, left); EdithFotografeert: 142 (top row, 4th); Elliotte Rusty Harold: 100 (bottom), 240 (bottom box, top); Ernest A Ross: 135 (7th row, 3rd), 250 (top row 2nd), 255 (top row, 1st); Emi: 137 (top row, 3rd), 140 (top left), 188 (top row, 3rd), 192 (top), 198 (top row, 4th), 263 (top row, 3rd and 4th); Feng Yu: 8, 99 (bottom left); Fortgens Photography: 257 (top row, 3rd); FotoRequest: 96 (top), 106 (second row, center), 106 (third row, right), 123 (bottom right), 134 (7th row, 1st), 135 (4th row, 1st), 170 (top right), 184 (top right), 204 (bottom row, right), 206 (bottom left), 209 (bottom row, 2nd), 217 (top right), 218 (top row, left), 218 (2nd row, right), 256 (top row 1st), 280 (3rd), 282 (2nd row, right); Fremme: 7 (top), 27 (top); George Sandu: 144 (bottom left); Gerald A. DeBoer: 135 (6th row, 1st), 222 (top row 1st), 226 (top row, 1st); Gerald Marella: 38 (bottom right), 65 (top left), 164 (2nd row, left), 177 (bottom row, 1st), 185 (top left), 252, (bottom), 264 (top row, 2nd); Ginger Livingston Sanders: 275 (1st); Glass and Nature: 29 (bottom stacked, bottom), 45 (top right), 123 (top right), 273 (1st); Glenn Price: 134 (4th row, 3rd), 176 (bottom row, 4th), 177 (top row, 3rd), 187 (top), 188 (top row, 1st), 190 (top left); GlenroyBlanchette: 145 (bottom); Golubev Dmitrii: 143 (top row, 4th), 147 (top); gregg williams: 152 (center right), 235 (bottom), 257 (top row, 1st); Hanjo Hellmann: 143 (bottom row, 3rd), 149 (top left); Ian Maton: 134 (2nd row, 1st), 135 (3rd row, 2nd), 138 (bottom), 161 (top row, left), 209 (top row, 2nd), 212 (top row, 1st), 216 (2nd row, right), 244 (top row, 1st), 246 (top row, center); Jack Nevitt: 132 (2nd from top); James Horning: 40 (bottom right); James.Pintar: 141 (right stacked, center); Jarrod Erbe: 37; JasonYoder: 265 (top row, 3rd), 283 (3rd); Jean-Edouard Rozey: 159 (bottom); Jeffrey Schwartz: 151 (top row, 1st); JiJaJuNg: 142 (top row, 1st); Jim and Lynne Weber: 224 (top right); Jim Nelson: 256 (bottom row, 1st), 259 (top center) 260 (top center); Jody Ann: 107 (bottom), 142 (top row, 2nd); Joe McDonald: 272 (2nd); Johannes Dag Mayer: 279 (2nd); John Drummond: 53 (center right); John E Heintz Jr: 36 (bottom right), 38 (bottom stacked, top); John L. Absher: 118, 135 (7th row, 4ht), 135 (10th row, 4th), 176 (bottom row, 3rd), 181 (top row, 1st), 250 (top row, 3rd), 254 (2nd row, left), 266 (top row, left), 268 (top left), 276 (3rd); K Quinn Ferris: 89, 99 (top); Karen Blaugrund: 165 (bottom); Kat Grant Photographer: 120 (top left), 123 (top left), 263 (bottom); Kathy Clark: 38 (top); KellyNelson: 9 (top), 241 (bottom); Keneva Photography: 154 (bottom), 154 (top left), 282 (3rd row, right); kenhartlein: 134 (3rd row, 2nd), 146 (top left); Kenneth Rush: 283 (top row, left); Kimberley McClard: 141 (bottom); Laura Mountainspring: 135 (10th row, 1st), 159 (center left), 244 (top row, 4th), 247 (top row, left); LaurieSH: 128; Lisa Stoorza: 122 (center right); Lloyd Wallin Photography: 131 (right), 165 (center left); Lois McCleary: 191 (bottom); Lorraine Swanson: 135 (5th row, 1st), 207 (top row, 3rd), 220 (top left); Lux Blue: 275 (4th); Marcin Perkowski: 140 (bottom); Maria Jeffs: 136 (top row, 4th), 138 (center row, center); Martha Marks: 41 (top right), 55 (top), 65 (top right), 192 (top left), 194 (center row, right), 196 (top right), 237 (top row, center), 266 (2nd row, left), 281 (1st); Matt Filosa: 134 (2nd row, 3rd); Matthew Orselli: 250 (top row, 1st); Max Allen: 229 (top row, 1st), 233 (top left); Melinda Fawver: 134 (9th row, 1st), 174 (top left); Melody Mellinger: 100 (top); Michael G. Mill: 162 (center row, center); Michael J Thompson: 135 (9th row, 3rd), 226 (top row, 4th), 281 (2nd); Michael Tatman: 35 (bottom left); Michael Woodruff: 179 (center left), 193 (top row, 2nd); Mike Truchon: 6 (top), 36 (bottom center), 135 (6th row, 4th), 251 (top row, 1st), 252 (top left); Mike_O: 6 (center), 35 (bottom center), 79, 82 (bottom); miker: 31 (top right); Mircea Costina: 19, 29 (bottom), 90 (top), 120 (center right), 122 (bottom right), 134 (3rd row, 4th), 134 (6th row, 3rd); 157 (2nd), 163 (top left), 177 (bottom row, 2nd), 184 (center), 189 (bottom row, left), 193 (top row, 3rd), 193 (bottom right), 195 (bottom), 206 (top row, 4th), 209 (top row, 3rd), 209 (bottom row, 1st), 215 (bottom box, bottom row, left), 220 (top center); Miroslav Hlavko: 124 (bottom); mlorenz: 167 (top row, 1st); moosehenderson: 166 (top row, 4th), 171 (bottom); Nancy Bauer: 7 (center), 23 (bottom), 121 (bottom right), 167 (top row, 3rd), 170 (bottom), 218 (bottom); Nina B: 134 (8th row, 1st), 172 (center); Norman Bateman: 30 (bottom center), 177 (top row, 2nd); Pacific Northwest Photo: 134 (5th row, 2nd), 164 (top row, left); passSy: 74 (left); Paul Broadbent: 142 (top row, 3rd); Paul Reeves Photography: 6 (bottom), 41 (top left), 54 (top right), 63 (bottom), 63 (center), 106 (2nd row, right), 120 (top right), 120 (bottom left), 131 (left),

134 (7th row, 3rd and 4th), 134 (5th row, 4th), 160 (center row, right), 166 (bottom), 174 (top right), 188 (top row, 4th), 189 (top row, 1st); 189 (bottom row, center and right), 193 (top row, 1st), 195 (top), 196 (top left), 199 (top row, 1st), 204 (top right), 205 (top row, right), 220 (center row, 1st), 223 (top row, 4th), 225 (top center), 229 (top row, 3rd), 230 (top row, 4th), 231 (top row, 1st), 234 (top), 235 (top right), 236 (bottom row, 2nd and 4th), 237 (top row, left), 241 (center left), 244 (top row, 3rd), 244 (bottom), 246 (2nd row, left), 251 (top row, 4th), 252 (top center), 256 (bottom row, 2nd), 260 (bottom), 261 (top row, 4th), 268 (top center), 282 (top row, right and left), 286 (bottom right), 287 (bottom right); Paul Sparks: 36 (center), 257 (top row, 4th); pcnorth: 121 (top right), 135 (4th row, 2nd), 176 (top row, 4th), 180 (bottom right), 217 (top left), 223 (top row, 1st), 227 (top left); Philip Rathner: 160 (bottom), 227 (top right); Phoo Chan: 288 (top left and right); Pi-Lens: 122 (center left); Pictureguy: 30 (top); QuinnKeon: 84 (bottom); Ramona Edwards: 9 (bottom); Randall Vermillion: 33 (bottom); Randy R: 185 (top right); raulbaenacasado: 190 (top right), 207 (bottom row, 3rd), 219 (top row, 2nd and 3rd); rck_953: 164 (top row, right), 236 (bottom row, 1st); Richard Guijt Photography: 156 (2nd), 159 (top left); RLHambley: 132 (bottom), 256 (bottom row, 3rd); Robert J Richter: 147 (center left); Robert L Kothenbeutel: 134 (4th row, 4th), 134 (9th row, 4th), 135 (3rd row, 1st), 164 (top row, center), 187 (center left), 198 (top row, 3rd), 202 (top right), 207 (top row, 1st and 4th), 216 (top row, left), 222 (top row, 3rd) 226 (top row, 2nd), 231 (bottom row, 3rd), 243 (top left), 258 (center left), 278 (3rd row, left); Ron Lam: 174 (bottom); Ron Rowan Photography: 163 (center row, left); Ronnie Howard: 134 (4th row, 1st), 150 (top row, 2nd), 152 (top right); Ronny Wolf: 280 (4th); Russell Watkins: 111 (left); Ryan S Rubino: 222 (top row, 4th), 226 (top row, 6th); Sarah Jessup: 165 (top); Sari ONeal: 30 (bottom right), 231 (bottom row, 4th), 243 (top right); SariMe: 75 (bottom left); Serguei Koultchitskii: 163 (center right); shaftinaction: 99 (bottom stack, bottom); Sharon Day: 120 (center left), 164 (2nd row, center); ShaunWilkinson: 70 (top right); Simonas Minkevicius: 199 (top row, 4th); Stacey Ann Alberts: 30 (bottom left); Steve Brigman: 262 (top); Steve Byland: 28 (bottom left), 40 (bottom left), 41 (bottom), 65 (bottom), 110 (bottom), 134 (5th row, 1st); 134 (6th row, 1st), 134 (8th row, 3rd); 135 (2nd row, 1st), 135 (5th row, 4th), 135 (9th row, 4th), 160 (center row, center), 162 (center row, left), 163 (center row, right), 171 (left stacked, bottom), 183 (bottom), 194 (top left), 198 (top row, 1st), 200 (center right), 200, top), 202 (top left), 206 (top row, 1st), 208 (top row, 2nd), 213 (top left), 214 (top right and left), 215 (bottom box, top row, right), 223 (top row, 3rd), 225 (top left), 231 (top row, 4th), 240 (top center), 245 (bottom row, 3rd), 248 (top left), 255 (top row, 4th), 259 (top left), 260 (top left); Steve Heap: 75 (bottom center), Steve Oehlenschlager: 125 (center); Steven R Smith: 123 (center left), 134 (1st row, 3rd), 161 (center row, center), 177 (top row, 1st), 183 (top), 215 (bottom box, bottom row, right), 228 (top row, 3rd and 4th), 232 (top row, 2nd and 4th); Stubblefield Photography: 29 (bottom stacked, top), 92 (center), 106 (3rd row, center), 143 (bottom row, 1st), 195 (center left), 203 (bottom), 252 (top right), 271 (4th), 282 (bottom row, right); sumikophoto: 124 (top); Svitlyk: 42 (top left); Takahashi Photography: 189 (top row, 4th), 194 (center row, center); TalyaPhoto: 74 (right); Tathoms: 234 (center left); teekaygee: 135 (6th row, 3rd), 231 (bottom row, 1st), 242 (top right); Thomas Morris: 151 (top row, 2nd), 273 (4th); Thorsten Spoerlein: 272 (1st); Tim Zurowski: 121 (center right), 122 (top left), 134 (2nd row, 4th), 134 (5th row, 3rd), 134 (10th row, 1st and 2nd), 135 (5th row, 2nd), 135 (7th row, 2nd), 135 (9th row, 1st and 2nd), 135 (10th row, 3rd), 136 (top row, 1st and 2nd), 138 (center row, left), 138 (top right), 143 (top row, 1st), 155 (top row, 4th), 157 (3rd and 4th), 170 (top left), 173 (top row, right), 176 (top row, 1st and 3rd), 176 (bottom row, 1st), 177 (bottom row, 3rd), 178 (top center), 179 (top), 180 (top), 181 (top row, 2nd and 3rd), 186 (top left), 188 (top row, 2nd), 189 (top row, 2nd), 191 (top), 191 (center left), 193 (top row, 4th), 197 (top), 206 (top row, 2nd and 3rd), 208 (top row, 3rd and 4th), 209 (top row, 1st), 215 (bottom box, center row, left), 215 (bottom box, top row, left), 215 (top center), 216 (top row, right and center), 221 (center left), 221 (top), 228 (top row, 2nd), 228 (bottom), 229 (top row, 2nd and 4th), 230 (bottom row, 4th), 231 (bottom row, 2nd), 231 (top row, 2nd), 232 (top row, 5th), 233 (top right), 237 (2nd row, left), 238 (top row, 2nd), 238 (bottom row, 3rd), 239 (top right), 241 (top), 242 (top left), 243 (top center), 245 (bottom row, 1st and 2nd), 245 (top row, 2nd), 247 (top row, right), 249 (center left), 249 (top), 256 (top row, 4th), 257 (bottom row, 2nd), 257 (top row 2nd), 261 (top row, 5th), 264 (top row, 4th), 264 (bottom), 265 (top row, 1st and 4th), 266 (2nd row, right), 270 (1st and 2nd), 271 (2nd and 3rd), 274 (4th), 275 (2nd), 275 (3rd), 278 (1st), 278 (3rd row, right), 278 (4th row, right and left), 280 (1st and 2nd), 281 (3rd and 4th), 282 (2nd row, left), 283 (2nd row, right and left), 283 (bottom), 284 (1st and 2nd); Tom Reichner: 121 (top left), 121 (bottom left), 132 (top), 132 (3rd from top), 134 (2nd row, 2nd), 135 (8th row, 3rd), 137 (top row, 1st and 4th), 139 (top right), 140 (top right), 150 (top row, 4th), 151 (top row, 3rd), 155 (top row, 3rd), 166 (top row, 1st), 186 (bottom), 249 (bottom right), 258 (bottom right), 272 (4th), 274 (1st), 277 (4th), 289 (bottom); Tony Campbell: 134 (8th row, 2nd), 167 (to row, 2nd), 173 (top row, left), 199 (bottom), 205 (bottom), 218 (top row, right); Tory Kallman: 137 (bottom), 141 (right stacked, bottom); Travel_Master: 142 (bottom), 144 (bottom-right stacked, bottom); TTshutter: 125 (top); UniquePhotoArts: 86 (bottom); vagabond54: 107 (top), 135 (5th row, 3rd), 268 (bottom right), 273 (2nd), 279 (3rd row, left); valleyboi63: 32 (top), 221 (bottom); Vern Faber: 286 (top right); Warren Price Photography: 26 (top). 32 (bottom), 35 (top left), 40 (top), 171 (left stacked, center); Wayne Morris: 52 (right); Wild Art: 134 (1st row, 2nd), 289 (top); wildphoto3: 226 (bottom box, left); Wilfred Marissen: 121 (center left); xpixel: 135 (8th row, 2nd), 209 (bottom row, 4th), 210 (top row, right); Zoran Karapancev: 210 (top row, center).

Index

(**bolded** page numbers are ID pages)